MW00984114

MAN BEFORE GOD

ADRIENNE VON SPEYR

Man Before God

Translated by Nicholas J. Healy
and D. C. Schindler

IGNATIUS PRESS   SAN FRANCISCO

Title of the German original:
Der Mensch vor Gott
© 1966 by Johannes Verlag, Einsiedeln

Cover art: *Crucifixion*
Panel of Sauvagnat (Puy-de-Dome), France.
Réunion des Musées Nationaux / Art Resource, NY
Cover design: Riz Boncan Marsella

ISBN 978-0-89870-882-0
Library of Congress Control Number 2005926543
Printed in the United States of America ∞

Contents

Limit and Its Overcoming

a. Nothingness and Limit

There comes a moment in every man's life when he begins to reflect on his place in the whole of the cosmos, on his future, and on the limits of what he can do. But he cannot think about his future without making his past part of the present moment. He sees what he has planned and achieved so far; he also sees everything that has not been achieved, the failed remainder, which perhaps stands before him as his own failure. He remembers days of work, days of rest, his nights, his daydreams, the great deal that he has received, and the little that he has given. He sees that it will not be easy to balance the books because so many seeds have not borne fruit. Many entries are left with question marks next to them; occasionally there is a successful item that could be marked with a round figure. And yet, it is not at all clear that this figure is really round; it is part of a series along with so many other figures that do not come out right.

And now man plans. He draws conclusions from his experiences. He wants to reach farther and different goals. But suddenly he hesitates: whatever plan he makes, he must always reckon with himself. He cannot envision any future that fully satisfies him, because he cannot count on any full performance from himself. He knows himself well enough to realize that he will always be an obstacle to himself because he does not remain faithful to his best resolutions. Wherever he turns, he encounters his limits. And yet he must go on, and he cannot do this unless he has before him a road, a destination, an image of his future—unless he undertakes something that satisfies him and that he brings about by his own power.

Once again he looks back on his past. He attempts to take a sober look at the obstacles that he himself placed on the path, to draw up an account of all that he has neglected. He tries to do this in a spirit in which he calls things by name and perceives the truth about the forces at work. None of this is easy, because as soon as he gives these failures their real name, he becomes painfully aware of his own responsibility. This failure humiliates him, and now things might seem darker to him than they really are. His confidence in the future wavers. He realizes how much remains undone; how often something was tried, abandoned, and forgotten again. The very first difficulty threw him off track; he simply gave up.

The past weighs on him and paralyzes his new resolutions. He knows beforehand that it will not work. He looks around in search of heroes who made up their minds to do some great work and did not let anything keep them from it. He would gladly be such a person, with the corresponding strength, ability, and perseverance. There is no end to his wishes and yearnings, but resignation debilitates them. He knows that, when all is said and done, he is no hero. Everything about him is futile.

It may occur to him that there are also Christian heroes. In their lives things really have been performed and accomplished, things whole and holy. If we examine more closely what they have done, if we try to penetrate into the mechanism of their achievement, we find aspects that can be understood together with a great deal that remains opaque. And yet the deed stands there in its rounded integrity, and it is impossible to detect any seams in it. This is curious, disturbing, and unsettling. From where does this unity come? Suddenly it becomes clear: In the Christian hero, the saint, man's nothingness is overcome. It has been absorbed into holiness. This indivisibility is grace, and it comes from God. God takes care of his own to the point of completely enveloping and covering them with his grace. But they are not buried underneath it, and they do not lose their distinctive face; they are not paralyzed by the weight of an excessive giving. Rather grace permeates, saturates, and sets aglow their entire being and places them in a new physical condition. Grace unites itself to man's innermost being; it produces in the saint, as it were, an incarnation that reenacts the Incarnation of the divine Son. Christ is God who became man in order to perform as God-man his integral, seamless deeds. The saint is a graced man and is permitted to perform equally integral deeds. By God's arrangement and action, grace and man have become a single reality. The resulting work retains the properties of both—those of man and those of grace—but forever united.

Whoever considers this successful outcome understands that man's nothingness represents a state of deficiency. Man lacks something. His sin has moved him away from the place where he should and could stand. He can, of course, fool himself into thinking that through sin he merely has strayed onto a bypath from which he still sees the right way. But deep down he knows better. He no longer sees the right way. He has become entangled in a thicket that his eye can no longer pierce in any way. Reflection alone cannot help him find the way out. He does not know how best to use his remaining strength. He needs grace for this, and therefore he must first of all submit. He must make himself so light that grace outweighs everything else in him. He must forget himself—this is the only true conclusion that follows from the recognition of his nothingness—in order to allow grace to stream into the empty space that he is.

As far as he is concerned, then, he is incapable of imitating the Christian hero. He cannot set off on his own to follow him. And nevertheless the image remains, the example with its radiant, inviting appeal. On the one side, he stands with his failure, his doubts, and with the need to make plans for his life that he knows he cannot sustain. On the other side stands the round deed of the apostolic man that shines upon him, challenges him, and fascinates him. Yet he realizes that he cannot leap over the intervening gulf by imitating from this side the deeds of a person who is on the other side. Rather he must get out of himself. The first comprehensive deed concerns the "I" itself. He must go out of himself; he must step outside of his own self. And this is a sort of annihilation, a forgetting and a losing of himself, and a call for a new solitude. It is a bursting of his own center in order to free up space for God, who enters into this center and from there makes something new out of him. Who above all takes him into his service. This possession must become the unifying point in him, but he will not be able to occupy, fix, or experience this point himself. He is catapulted out of the limits of this nothingness, but he cannot trace this described trajectory, because he has surrendered and lost himself.

All at once the word "nothingness" acquires a new meaning for him; it is now nothing more than a signal, a warning sign.

b. The Removal of Limits in Christ

When man knows about God and experiences his own limitedness, the vanity of his efforts, and the insurmountableness of the obstacles that are placed before him, then these experiences of his limits become an indication for him of a beyond. His passing time becomes for him the sign of God's eternity; his barriers, the sign of infinity. Thanks to his limits, he is kept constantly reminded and warned. And yet, his human capabilities and experiences, for all their limitedness, do not stand in opposition to what God is and is capable of. After all, God created man in his image, and an image cannot be in contradiction to what it represents. What is contradictory, what is next to incomprehensible about man, what cuts short every comparison, is sin. Sin has turned man's eyes away from the original model, detached his life from God, and plunged him into solitude.

The Son of God assumes human nature just as he happens to find it, with the consequences of sin, but without sin. He overcomes the weariness that he feels after long travels and night watches by the strength of a human obedience to God. This obedience cannot simply be regarded as a power that he takes over from his divinity. He does not allow himself the freedom of constantly elevating his assumed human nature beyond its limits. He puts up with more than others because he loves more; he endures more because he is more obedient. He gives us this love and this obedience so that we can learn not to stumble continually over our limits but rather to stretch them a little in order to serve God better and fulfill more adequately the task he has set for us. But here below, this overcoming of one's limits occurs little by little. It is not, for instance, the beginning of a gradual conquest of the laws of the body by the spirit or a systematic displacement of our limits in the direction of infinity. For humility, patience, and the love that bears all things are virtues that God has bound together with our limits and our experience of limits. How could someone who managed constantly to overleap his own limits still be humble? How could someone be patient if impatience always spurred him to further successful achievements? There is a measure that is laid on us. We can use this measure only (as a gift) in love for God, rather than inordinately grasping it for ourselves. This measure, which is entrusted into God's hands (as is our nullity), not only makes us newly aware of our finitude, but it also makes us forget ourselves and feel secure within God's embrace, in the very way that the Son revealed to us through his human existence. Perhaps no one was ever so lonely as he was during his forty-day fast in seclusion and temptation. And yet this solitude flows back into solidarity with us. It was not a severance of every connection; rather, it was a task of love, and love never separates; it unites even when desert and solitude are the means of achieving unity. Whoever saw him there would have seen only that he was alone. However, he took us with him into his prayer; we are there with him. His Holy Spirit has overcome all the limits of our own spirit—our being here and not there. We are carried and taken along by the Son and thus are no longer "here and not there"; rather, we are "both here and there at once". The perception that we are "here and not there" is a function of our reason, which is bound to human laws. Through our know-it-all attitude we often impose a finitude on our understanding and love by speaking the word "impossible" whenever we experience our limits. What we set down as physically impossible—"I can only keep going or stay awake for so many hours"—is already overcome in the Spirit of the Lord. Consequently, we do not need to waste any time on it, and we should not think and talk incessantly about our limits. Ever since God became man, we have been able to find the unlimited within our limitations.

We can imagine, for example, that we have reached the limit of our power to stay awake and thus are no longer able to say a certain prayer that we had made up our mind to recite. We can then recommend this prayer in faith to God and his saints. Angels can pray it for us, and God can also hear our good intention and grant it; he can make us understand that we have been heard, regardless of the fact that we "know for certain" that we did not say the prayer ourselves. As a matter of fact, it may be that God prefers to have the power of our prayer and of all that we undertake in his name begin precisely at the point at which we have run up against our limits, that point at which we have become too weary in his service—wherever that may be—to bring to completion what we would have liked. Christ suffered this "not being able to carry on" to the point of death. Death was the limit of this incapacity, and he went to this limit. He did not set the limit of his death himself; he would have gone as far beyond the limit of death as the Father willed. And precisely at the limit of death the salvation of the world begins, and the perfect fulfillment of the Father's will emerges into view. God's victory came at the limit of death. His absolute infinity breaks through at the point of our absolute finitude.

Consequently, all the limits that we know from our existence, or, in another way, from the existence of Christ, are landmarks. Humanly speaking we would say: Here we run into a stone wall. Here is where our property stops and our neighbor's field begins. The landmarks placed in fields mark property lines. However, when it is a question of spiritual property, such demarcations are no longer valid; rather, they have been abolished. What is mine is also yours and his. There is the communion of saints, the Church, in which the Lord shows something of the limit-lessness of his divinity and the eternity of his love. In this realm one can pray and sacrifice in place of another, or both can do the same work together. One can be "done" in the other, just as we are redeemed in the temptation of Jesus or in his Cross and just as the twelve-year-old Messiah truly burst through the boundaries for us on the way to the Father and made it possible for us to follow after him. The Church is the place where all limited beings are gathered to-gether in freedom from limitation. Insofar as their limits are removed, they are in principle saints. In-sofar as they live in accord with this freedom from limitation, they also bring to fulfillment the holiness that has been granted them.

c. Living beyond Our Limits

The Christian who becomes aware of his limits faces them from two points of view, one practical and the other theoretical. Practically speaking, he is called upon to overcome his own limits in the sense of believing in the unlimitedness of God. Of course, there exists a realm beyond our capabilities, a realm to which we no longer have access. But as Chris-tians we must not mark out our field of activity with the boundary stones of what seems "possible". This means, however, that our "self-knowledge" cannot be the decisive factor. We have to act as if we were spec-ulatively gifted; we have to consider the impossible alongside the possible and the limitless next to the limited. If we had to rely solely on ourselves and our self-knowledge, we would, when facing a task, prudently and anxiously fix the boundaries more closely. We would prefer the smaller job that is easy to oversee and that we can guarantee to get done. But if we are believers who are aware of the power of prayer, the Church, substitution, and the communion of saints, then we push the boundaries of our assigned task a bit farther. We place more trust, not in ourselves, but in grace and in the Church that accompanies us. First we have to acknowledge the measure meted out to us; then we have to forget it. For we can no longer trust ourselves to measure our own capacities. This does not mean, of course, that we should devise wild plans and put them into action. But we can plan in conjunction with prayer in the Holy Spirit, without fixing him or us. What is important is our direction, commitment, and attitude. Looking toward God, we attempt to perform the tasks that have been set before us in the attitude of believers. What subsequently results, how much we accomplish on our own power, how much the Holy Spirit does in us, how far the boundaries of nature have been moved—these are things that we do not need to know. It is enough for us to know that they have been moved in the direction of God. No one could accept any apostolic mission in the Church, no one could so much as dispense the sacraments, if he did not know that he performed only a fraction of the act and that it is the

Holy Spirit who, in the realm of the Lord's Church, does all that can be expected in faith. This consideration and its application can be taken as a maxim for action whenever there is some practical work to be done.

There is also the theoretical side: In what do the task and the efficaciousness of prayer consist? Such things are much harder to determine. A Carmelite nun enters the convent in order to make atonement for the sin of the world. If she thinks about it realistically, she realizes how unbelievably small her contribution will be. She prays distractedly; here and there she oversteps the rule in trivial matters. She feels herself to be a sinner and knows that her sin impedes the working of grace. In spite of that, she prays the prescribed amount every day, does various works of penance, helps where she can—and all the while sees the futility of her action and the nullity of her endeavors. If before her death she looks back at her life, she recognizes that despite everything the main thing was right, because at bottom she wanted to give herself to God. She recognizes that she has been sustained by many, by the prayer of her sisters (those of today and of yesterday), and by the founders of the order. She recognizes that she owes her life in the order to the prayers of all the saints, to the intercession of the Mother of God, to the grace of the Lord and the triune God, indeed, even to the many sinners for whom she supposed she had sacrificed herself and given herself up. What has proved to be the theme of her life ultimately stems, not from her, but from others. She has been carried along and sustained beyond the limits of her own nullity.

Only in extremely rare cases can a Christian see the fruits of his prayer so as to be able to say, for example, ''Thanks to my prayer or to yours this was prevented and that granted; this or that 'mountain' was moved.'' Nevertheless, from time to time we experience a miracle; something for which we had begged is granted, or the propitious turn of events for which we had hardly hoped actually occurs. Because in every prayer ''futility'' is overcome; because our limits vanish, and eternity manifests itself in time. And one who prays simultaneously experiences the invisibility of divine action, which weaves itself into and enlivens our prayer from within. Thus the futility and nullity of our today stands in the midst of the unshakableness and infinity of eternity, without our being aware of what is happening to us.

2

God's Life for Us

a. Underway to God

When man prays, he does not see his partner. He knows only that a dialogue is going on. Now, suppose it has been a long time since he last freshened up his prayer and that his prayer has shriveled. All that is left is an emergency prayer that he stammers out in dark moments or a prayer that he recites by rote because he remembers that, after all, prayer is part of being a Christian. If this is the case, then he will see himself as someone who pronounces something that in some way is perceived and taken notice of by God but that he himself does not hear, see, or imagine beyond the sound of his words. It is almost as if he were reciting a speech in an empty room addressed half to himself and half to the things around him. Wasted words. If he were completely alone, they might be words of vexation or words that he speaks aloud because he likes their sound, that he wants to reverberate inside him as a reminder of something. Or else, by talking he tries to revive someone else's words, but these words are nothing more than markers so as not to forget something. The speaker does not lend them an actual and personal significance. And no new meaning is disclosed in his talking. For this reason, it is finally irrelevant.

But if the man praying is a genuine believer who is aware of the significance of what he is doing, he knows that he is speaking in God's sight. He allows his word to reach his dialogue partner; he is thoroughly convinced that it is heard and understood and that it has an effect in God. Thus, seized with the greatness and omnipotence of God, he cannot help but sink down even farther on his knees. As if blinded, he looks into an overpowering light. All at once he gets an intimation of what God's life is. At first, perhaps, he sees only the life by which God administers and guides the world and providentially orders its course. Then in a deeper sense, he sees the eternal life as a triune exchange of love within God himself. This is a life that creates itself in love —a love that is both question and answer at once in an eternal circulation. And this circulation appears so full to the one praying that he could almost lose heart. He feels it would be improper to push his way in or, indeed, to interrupt just to say something himself. But he cannot deny that he was addressed, and so he has no choice but to remain in the attitude of prayer as long as God needs him. And since God does not limit the necessities of his love, neither can the one praying place any measure on them. He would have to pray without measure in order to grasp something of God's boundlessness. He would have to be able to suspend the limitations of his words so that they could enter into God's infinity. He would have to attempt, in whatever way, to conform his prayer time to eternity.

He will thus be compelled to pray in such a way that his prayer becomes *contemplation*. He must contemplate God's life. His point of access is the divine-human life of the Son as portrayed in the Gospel, which proceeds from the human life that opens and broadens itself to the Father and the Spirit; from finite, historical time into the endless duration of eternity. At the same time, he will know that the Son is accompanied and embraced by the Father and the Spirit, so that in the word of the Son he can enter more deeply into the life of the Trinity. The barriers that he feels dropping at that instant have never existed at all in the triune God. What from the earthly point of view looks like an obstacle does not exist when seen from God's perspective. What makes this man waver and hesitate, what stands in the way of his love, has from eternity already been overcome in the dialogue of the triune God. He is like a blind man who can take a few steps in a familiar room and who has arranged objects in the room to get his bearings, who now suddenly finds himself in a room without obstacles. He can step freely in any direction and no longer needs to keep to the routine he has learned.

But if, in spite of this, he feels for obstacles with his stick, he becomes uncertain because he cannot find them anymore. In similar fashion, the one who prays can suddenly become uncertain before God, because finitude has been pulled away. But this is a healing uncertainty that brings knowledge. All that has contributed to his "I"—everything spatial, temporal, and psychological—has vanished and will not have any replacement. No other obstacles, no other spaces or times or character traits are put in its place. A genuine void has to be formed so that God's fullness can pour into it. And yet this fullness is totally other than the void; it is not the counterpart or the contrary of the void, since God is not the contrary of the world, nor is fulfillment the contrary of the expectation. It is something "other"; it is the otherness of God, that overwhelming reality beyond all the creature hopes for and has the power to conceive. It is that absolutely unmistakable quality that upon arriving does not first have to prove that it is divine. This is the first characteristic of the divine life. When the Son of God becomes man, this is not a No coming out of a Yes, nor is No said to God so that Yes can be said to man. The Son does not disavow his divine nature by taking on his human nature. It is impossible to place either a plus or a minus sign before one or the other form of God—man, not-man. We can say only that in his humanity the fullness and his "otherness" become near and are revealed to believers. The Son is the Word of the Father and expresses this otherness of God in all that he is and does. Through him we become acquainted on earth with the mysteries of heaven. In him the kingdom of heaven has drawn near. But it has done so as that "other" which even in earthly circumstances and concepts does not cease to be other. Every time the Lord's parables begin with the words "The kingdom of heaven is like . . .", they wholly and reliably refer to this other. Therefore we cannot say that the succession of images in the parables exhaustively transposes the essence of the kingdom into worldly concepts. Taken by itself, each image is completely earthly, and if Christ were not the Word, it would never have occurred to anyone to find the otherness of heaven expressed in such images. The Son creates the relation through his reference, or, better, he creates it fundamentally by means of his Incarnation, whereby he himself becomes the reference. He becomes at once the way and the truth through which we obtain access to the life of God.

Accordingly, we must conform our partial truth to his truth and approximate our human life to the life of heaven through the human life of the Son. By having been created, we are already essentially on the way to the Son. For we were created for his sake and with him as our goal. Consequently, the measure of time and space is also with him, although this measure is unknown to us. What space, what time must we traverse in order to reach the Son? We know only that it is the time of our life, though we do not know the "hour". The space is the Church, but we cannot measure out this space. We were created to journey toward the Son for the duration of our lives, which we live out in the Church. But since we lack both measures, a new uncertainty comes over us: we feel ourselves suspended in the void. All that is ours enters into the mystery of God, even as it also comes forth from the mystery of God. God gives us all the necessary provisions for our pilgrimage, but the source of the giving remains in him, because he is love.

And this love of God who is other, this "other" love, remains so overwhelmingly great that everything we undertake to imitate it can be no more than an attempt. We are like children who try to imitate the gestures of adults, their father at work, for example. But this is play. We do not perform the action itself. The meaning of the father's gesture lies in his work. That the child does out of love something meaningless that the father does meaningfully is touching. In the same way, the man who loves God imitates something he sees God doing. He knows that his imitation is feeble and is meaningful only as an imitation of that which has all its meaning in God. The believer can do nothing else than show the Father in this way that he has understood something of the Son's reference and that he speaks a Yes to which God alone can give content and fullness.

b. Imitation of the Inimitable

No one can separate what is knowable about God from what is not, so that what is knowable can be put into pure concepts. When Christ refers to God's heavenly kingdom by his words and his life, he points to the otherness of God, which always remains a mystery. And yet *as* mystery, God's otherness approaches us and reveals itself to us, offering itself to us in faith so that we may participate and follow as disciples.

It is a participation in mystery, as our participation in Christ in the Eucharist clearly shows. He is present in innumerable churches around the world, offering himself to be eaten and to be adored. It is always different hosts, made from different bread, which comes from different fields, prepared by different men. Yet this bread is consecrated by the same words of consecration and so enters into the unity of the same presence. The Hosts are distributed by completely different priests to completely different members of the faithful: the one divine life that the Lord contains for the world flows into the plurality of the world in order to give it unity. Indeed, this life gathers the plurality of the world into itself in order to distribute the unified world, too, into the plurality of the world every time it distributes itself.

And the goal of the communication of Christ in the Eucharist is discipleship. Its origin lies in the Son's following the Father's will throughout his earthly life in order to make the divine life a reality on earth. Thus, discipleship has its origin in a life of renunciatory love that is obedient and poor unto death as well as virginal, that is, exclusively at the Father's disposition. What the Lord later formulated in his "evangelical counsels" is, at its core, his own following of God. He fulfills therein the faith of the Old Testament: existence in obedience to the word of God wherever it leads. However, the idea that discipleship also includes imitation is conceivable only after the Word has become flesh, making possible a human communion of life. Yet the discontinuity unveils itself once again precisely in this nearness. To follow Christ and to imitate him means to choose what is inimitable, incomparable, and unrepeatable as the guiding rule of one's life—to choose the perfection that he is and that we will never be able to be.

Disheartened, we *can* run to the Mother of the Lord. She is human like us. She spoke her Yes, worshipped, and gave herself away in love. She accompanied the Son in faith all the way to the Cross in order at the very last to pass into the form of the Church. Yet her *fiat* towers above ours. She was uniquely chosen to be the vessel of the Holy Spirit, for a fruitfulness in faith that is bodily efficacious and thus inimitable for all of us. Mary's mission is unique and will not be given a second time to any one of us.

In the distance between Mary's mission and ours, it finally becomes clear that this is always a distance that allows for nearness and following. Rejoicing over the uniqueness of our Mother's mission, we realize that every fruitfulness in the Church is made possible by her fruitfulness. A fruitfulness that shares in hers can carry the Son as the Word in faith and loving surrender, in prayer and apostolate, in order to allow him to become flesh in us and in the world. And by participating in Mary's fruitfulness, we are trained in the Son's own following, in his Yes to the Father and his renunciatory love. This discontinuity between him and us, which threatened to discourage us, has been, so to speak, neutralized. The distance reveals itself clearly and reassuringly to be the precondition for our nearness to the Lord. And if we fall short of our mission, as we constantly do, within the Son's and Mother's full completion of their task, our lives nevertheless will take after theirs, so that we may receive through both a share in the life of God.

And since the two things, the Eucharist and discipleship, are intermeshed, we do not remain standing at a distance before God's otherness in the way that the image stands before the threshold of the reality. Through Communion, God's reality and truth in Christ enter into us and give us the gift of God's life, by which we are allowed to carry out the act of discipleship. Looking back at the Old Covenant, we realize how efficacious God's word already was in enabling man to have an existence in faith and in showing him God's vitality, which in a hidden way already presupposes a triune life of love. Yet only in the New Covenant, and essentially through the Son's eucharistic self-donation, is this vitality of God revealed as what it is: an eternal exchange of love. And since this life is now offered to us so that we, too, can make it the substance of our life, the Yes and the act of faith first attain the breadth to embrace the whole of human life. The form of Christ's life (especially in the evangelical counsels) really becomes the formative power of our own lives. Only now can the Church—in contrast to the synagogue—be apostolic in her very essence. What the hidden life of God himself is, is revealed in the life of Christians. And this life of Christians becomes the indispensable mediating organ for the self-presentation of God in his world.

c. Our Redemption in the Son

As the Creator of the world, God the Father eternally knows that he will have to retrieve sinful humanity, and the Son stands eternally ready for the work of redemption as its guarantor. He will give the Father those who love him by incorporating them into his redemptive work. No one can attain to true love of God without the help of the Son. Only in Christ is it revealed to the world how God loves; only in him is man made pure enough for this love to take possession of him.

In Christ God becomes man: a man who at first sight is no different from other men but whose statements about himself go beyond anything a man can say about himself. He is inseparably the Word and Son of the Father, and he is incarnate as both. When the Father speaks with the Son as his Word, he is addressing man. When the Son answers the Father, he addresses the Father in his incarnate Person together with man. This conversation is not split into two parts; you cannot say: Up to here is what the Father has to say to the Son, and then comes what he has to say to man; and, up to here is what man says to God, and then comes what the Son has to say to the Father. Rather, man hears in the Son the whole word of the Father and joins in speaking the whole word of the Son to the Father. As the *one* Word, the Son incorporates into himself every one of man's prayers and words. And yet the power of the Word that is turned toward man lies in the power of the Word that is addressed to the Father. What the Son says to the Father is the substance of what he says as an apostle sent into the world. From now on it is unthinkable that the Son could speak with the Father without bearing in himself the Father's creation and returning it to him, without worshipping the Father as Creator along with all creatures and placing in this worship his entire filial love, which is simultaneously for the Father and for the Father's work. This one yet twofold movement is that of the one Word, who in

God knows no limits but on whom his human form
seemingly places limitations. Christ speaks to his disciples, and the word does not reach beyond the small
circle in which it is audible. But because it is divine,
it does not lose the limitlessness of eternity when it
enters the limitedness it assumes as a result of the
Incarnation. It is charged with the undiminished divine meaning. It is, not a partial truth, but a vessel
of the whole divine truth; it is therefore a truth that
goes beyond every meaning man allows to truth. It
is the "beyond" in itself, boundless and eternal. No
word spoken by the Son loses its meaning over time.
It is always a redemptive word. If a man is asked
how he understands his salvation, he will be able to
present a few aspects: he is set free from the sin under which he suffered; he sees before him a realm of
freedom into which he can enter; he can become a
new man. However, these and similar aspects can all
be understood only within the realm of the Cross.
But who understands the Cross? "I thirst", cries the
Son. His agonizing thirst is, in its depths, the thirst of
the Son for the Father, the thirst to lay in the Father's
hands the completed world—a world that not only
is loved, but also loves. It is the thirst to see a world
in which nothing is ever turned against the Father
again; the thirst to experience love from all men so
as to be able to redirect it to the Father. This experience lies in the Son; it has its place where he rises and
reaps the fruit of his Passion. But because he eternally

desires to redeem the world, he also eternally has this redeemer's thirst to perform his task to the uttermost —to do the Father's will to the very end. And if his Resurrection to eternal life means a placation of this thirst, the Word, as incarnate, is always at work in the "now" of every time. He is a Word that is uttered and heard, that is taken to heart or rejected, and that ascends and returns. Therefore, as long as he remains and works on earth, he is also a Word who thirsts. He is full of longing to bring about more redemption. This eternal thirst of the Redeemer effects our redemption on the Cross through the carrying of all sins. Consequently, it remains actual as long as space and time still hold sinners whose sin has to be carried. During the Passion, this thirst intensifies: from the Mount of Olives to every lash and blow, to every nail driven in, to every second on the Cross, until it permeates the whole being of the suffering Lord. It continues beyond the cry "I thirst" into the ultimate weakness that can no longer speak but only die. And the Father allows all of the mysteries of suffering, which the Word experienced to the extreme, to return to the Father along with the Son when he raises him from the dead. The Father knows the Word so well that he need only touch him in secret in order to have him return to eternal life together with all his experiences of the world, sin, and hell. It is the Father's eternal Word who now bears within himself all the words of the world and of man. Through

the sending out of the Word, we have become believers; through his suffering, we have become new;
through his Resurrection, we have risen in the Word;
and through his homecoming to the Father, we too
speak the Son's word to the Father. And we do so in a
way that goes right to the Father's heart. For, thanks
to the Son's path, his Father has become our Father
as well. And since the Son's return took place in the
Holy Spirit, the Spirit is given to us at the moment
when the circle of love between the Father and the
Son closes again, this time right through the world.

Such is the immeasurable truth into which the concept of redemption opens up. Like any other concept
pertaining to the revelation of the Word, it cannot be
rounded out anywhere except in the eternal life of
the Trinity.

d. Living in God's Word

When two people bid each other farewell, a final
word is spoken. It remains in their hearts; they cul-
tivate and cherish it, keep its fire burning and are
themselves sustained by it. Their parting word seems
to hold the power to bridge over the chasm of separation and in the midst of absence to give life and to
pledge it. This word consequently becomes a task. If
those who are parting love each other, each one of
them wants the word to mold him in love, so that the
next meeting carries a sign and stamp of this word.

When God speaks the word, he puts something of his own life into it. And when the word crosses, as it were, the bounds of heaven and comes to earth, it does not forfeit this life; rather, it becomes the giver of life for every possible situation. It gets a hook into man in order to call his attention to God and God's will. Even more, it communicates to man the life that is in God's love. The Son on earth, while constantly beholding the Father, speaks of the Father and of his relation to him as well as of himself and his teaching. And he does all of this in obedience to the Father as the expression of his mission. He throws us the word like a ball that we have to catch. This calls for attention and consent; the Christian cannot content himself with acknowledging the event of having heard the word as a fact, which he then puts behind him. For the word contains more life than man himself. Indeed, it contains infinitely more than he can imagine. Even if it is abused, dismissed from the mind, lost, or forgotten, it remains the expression and evidence of God's love. As such it has the power to rekindle itself again and again into a blazing fire, to appear once more suddenly before man and make a claim on him. Everything that it demands has to do with life. It remains the expression of life in a way we can never suspect.

We may encounter the word in the liturgy, in the homily, or in the contemplation of Scripture, but the full meaning of the encounter always lies in the future: Love one another! The preached word is only a stimulus to action, and action is the way in which the believer gives back to God the word he has received. People who answer God in this way radiate a light that does not originate in them but shines from heaven through the word they have welcomed in faith. We can calculate how much light a young plant needs in order to unfold, but we cannot calculate how much light God must shine on his people in his word until they learn to unfold in the power of this light. This encounter in light leaves no room for choice, because God has already chosen all along. The man who entrusts himself to the light of the word is molded by it. It is as though he unfolds his branches, leaves, and flowers in the direction shown him by the light. And being oriented in this way by the light is ultimate *freedom*. Light does not coerce; it invites. Even where the light demands something, it does so as an invitation, as a presentation of new and better possibilities, as the offer of youthful strength to a weary life.

A No to the grace of the word is primarily a rejection of the life that God gives. Only secondarily is it also a self-deprivation on man's part. Man has so much freedom that he appears capable of keeping God's life at a distance. Of course, he cannot deprive God of his possibilities. It is not God who is restricted; it is man alone who narrows himself and thereby prevents the unfolding of that aspect of God's own vitality that he wanted to express in man. The parable of the sower expresses this truth: the seed falls on soil that does not allow it in. Nevertheless, we cannot say that God, if he is the sower, has lost his seed, because for God everything is possible. He can even make another seed sprout a hundredfold in place of the one seemingly lost seed. Yet there remains that place where man says No to the life of God. You can perhaps for a long time point to someone who denies the faith and whose naysaying seems to have had a great influence. But the naysayers can end up challenging the ones who say Yes and cause them to grow in number. They sense more deeply the vitality of God and search for ways to convey it to others.

The parables of the kingdom and its divine mysteries have to be understood, on the one hand, in the Spirit and, on the other hand, in their concreteness that man can grasp. Grasping and not grasping are often found very close together. You can grasp a certain layer of something, but behind that there remains what has not been comprehended. Scientists, for instance, who study the rudimentary forms of life, often push suddenly through one layer of the problem into a deeper one. It is not seldom that scientists then loudly proclaim that they have found the secret of life. But they have discovered only a new form or outward manifestation of life, whose origin still lies hidden behind it. The origin of God's word lies with the Father; from there it gets its entire heavenly vitality, which can never be grasped from the world's perspective. For the believer, it is possible to contemplate the word in light of its origin. Indeed, we can examine every word of the Lord—his words to his disciples and to sinners, to the indifferent and to the hostile—for what it reveals of its heavenly origin. God himself has mysteriously unveiled this origin of divine life: the origin is the love of the Father, who generates the word out of love and gives all words to us as a gift of love. Of course, one can also, so to say, catch the word along the way, running into it somewhere along its path. But when it is a question of its vitality, he will still have to trace it back to where it springs forth from the Father. The life of God reveals itself only in God, and only in faith can we reach back to this origin. It is not by a created power that we reach the origin, but because the Son sees and communicates the Father to us, and his word strikes us with his divine power.

3

Knowledge

a. The Misunderstood Word and the Understood Word

In prayer, man is united with God in a way that in many respects can be compared to a conversation. The person who prays speaks and receives an answer in faith; he asks, and his request is granted; he seeks, and he finds. In a conversation between individuals, there are surprises, especially when you still do not know your partner well. You size him up, think you have guessed the right topic and level, and act accordingly. But it may be that your conversation partner does not feel personally addressed and responds with things that have hardly anything to do with the subject. Or the contrary happens, and he is more deeply affected than you foresaw and makes a unique, decisive revelation that in its turn exceeds your expectation. And so you have to change everything. Or perhaps you know whom you have before you: the man is famous, and everyone knows his intelligence and his area of expertise. He also takes pains not to make you feel this distance too much and with simple words gives you a glimpse of things that you can understand but that are new to you. You believe that you have understood, and you are pleased with the conversation. You feel richer afterward; you try definitively to appropriate what you have learned, and, as circumstances permit, you pass it on as your own. You may do this in all honesty because you have forgotten where it came from or because everything was so luminously clear that you immediately took it as your own in order to go back to it at a suitable moment . . .

In conversation with God, a good deal happens that advances our knowledge of him. We get to know him with the help of what he communicates and tells us about himself. There are, to be sure, illusions: I can beg God in prayer for a certain answer, for example, to show me whether I should act one way or another. If, however, my own desire to do this and not that is very strong, then God's answer can easily be blocked. I do not give him a genuine chance to have his say; rather, I hear my own voice in an enlarged megaphone. In this case, nothing would be gained in the way of knowledge of God. Man pulled God to his own level and, still more, confused what he wanted to hear with what God had to say to him. But if prayer is really a conversation, then I have to come before God ready to let him speak, as if he were a very famous, infinitely superior partner who nevertheless deigns to make himself understandable to me. For since God wants to reach into the life of his believer in order to form him, he is also inclined to express what the believer absolutely must understand in such a way that he can grasp and appropriate it.

The average Christian often tends to look upon God as a sort of higher man whom he pictures according to his own understanding. He does not leave God the freedom to be completely different, to be infinitely greater and truly eternal. In his desire to understand God, he molds him according to his own ideas and views. Thus, without really ever noticing, he has already put what is divine about God behind him. Divinity is, in a sense, for him like one property among others, which he need not pay attention to or marvel at. If the Christian does not become aware of this danger in good time, he ends up standing before God like a know-it-all, and his prayer will lead him to the opposite of knowledge of God. In the lukewarmness of habitual prayers and in the superficiality that arises from returning to the same thing day after day and never renewing it, this supposed God will merely supply him with prepackaged answers— just like a machine. Almost without noticing, the one who prays thus becomes so arrogant that he believes that prayer is no longer needed. When something out of the ordinary comes up, for example, when it is plain to him that his own reason falls short, he will remember God and call to him. But he has forgotten how to leave God the freedom to intervene in his life in the way that God wants and to make a more profound believer out of him. Moreover, he no longer stands within discipleship. Everything is reduced to the barest simplicity, so that the most superficial truths, utterly bereft of any depth, are enough for him and, therefore, ought to be enough for God.

If, however, the one praying becomes conscious in reverence and love of his distance from God, if he loves God as he is in himself—whether he understands him or not—then he gives God the opportunity to reveal himself to him. He will learn something about God every time he prays. To be sure, this will not happen with lawlike regularity or according to clearly defined steps of knowledge. But thanks to God's gracious generosity, the one who prays will come to see more and more of him and will understand more and more intimately what God actually means to say to man. Every one of God's answers and every one of his demands will reveal a bit more of his essence to the believer. And what appears to the one contemplating, what comes into view and matures in prayer, will nourish his understanding of God's essence. For all that God communicates can, at least to a certain degree, be perceived and understood. God's words are never of such a kind that they immediately lead to a steep precipice and to the night in which absolutely nothing is comprehensible. God shows himself.

He shows himself in the word and in the language that the Son speaks to us. And because he invites man to follow him, he can also show himself in every human language. Each of them can become a vehicle of God and a pointer to him, to his ungraspable, holy word that is permeated by eternal love. In human speech, which is divided into single words and passes away, God says what abides forever and cannot be divided. Within the templates of human concepts, he says what is unique and ever new, what is just as true and urgent today as it was thousands of years ago. Truth has its home so deeply in the word of God that it appears nowhere more clearly and radiantly. And because the word is true insofar as it is God's word, it is *knowledge* leading into an ever-greater truth. Knowledge that comes from the word and goes back to it. There is no truth and no knowledge whose tendency is away from the word. By being spoken, the word shows in its truth what truth as such is. And this makes it a word that attracts man, lifts him up to himself, and transforms him in love. The word desires that all of man's action contains the sound of the divine voice and its truth.

It is certainly true that someone can quite suddenly become aware of God's presence. God stands before him and demands something definite. God can come upon the believer like a sudden fatal shock, like a bolt of eternal truth. A word is spoken to him, and everything that is not this word fades away without a trace. But for the most part, the word proceeds gingerly; it gradually unveils its presence to us, its ever-greater dimensions and uncompromising demands. Indeed, it can turn out to be even more demanding for man in this way. While the lightning bolt may appear to him like something incomprehensible, the gradual unveiling carries with it the slow dawning of knowledge from which there is no escape.

Personal, individual
b. *The Demand for Subjective Participation*

Knowledge is always insight into something; it is objective. In faith, however, knowledge of God acquires something more in relation to the subject and his existence. The matters pertaining to the content of faith are defined in precise terms by the Church. They are all things having to do with the knowledge of God and what he requires. But the Christian can distance himself from these things as if they were neutral objects. If, on the contrary, he understands that these dogmas are true *with reference to him*, are aimed at him, are meant to take possession of him, he must give up his former purely neutral consideration: faith demands the "I". Man has to enter with his entire subjectivity into the sphere of Christian truth. He cannot alter this truth, and yet it now changes for him, because henceforth it belongs to him, takes root in him, and in certain respects has become his reality. Thus he must now approach the truth on the basis of this reality. He will take notice of the processes of transformation going on in him, and he will be led to observe that it is always *he* who changes in conformity with the truth, and not vice versa. The subject is called to enter into the objectivity of faith so that this objectivity can actively penetrate the believer's entire existence. *Thus* will his knowledge, and his corresponding apostolic work and preaching, bear the stamp of his personality. He will proclaim the God whom he has encountered and come to know. Every believer, whoever he may be, will comport himself in this way. Nor does this impair the greatness and objectivity of God and of his revelation. It does not alter the faith; rather, it demonstrates that the Son's Incarnation has truly been able to bring God's truth into every "I" and to inflame in it love for the God of love.

To use an image: God is a blazing center toward whom people stream in confession and knowledge of him, like rays that stream from the periphery toward the center. Each starts from a different point, which need not be disowned, because all creatures originally streamed forth from the divine center and received from God an assigned place and characteristic nature from which to begin their return. This image indicates that in every case the believer is in movement, and is so toward a particular goal, namely, God. And the route he must traverse is a path of knowledge. Whoever looks into the sun is blinded; but the rays that he sees could, in and of themselves, just as well come from the sun as go toward it. When someone knows God, grace streams to him from the divine center in order to lead him back to that center. Corresponding to this movement of grace from God is man's movement to God in the form of knowledge.

If someone were to read through all the works of the countless people who have written about God and about what God meant for them and their path in life, it would soon become clear that all of them are saying essentially the same thing. Yet each of them wants to convince you through his own intimate experience. Each bears witness to the path that God intended for him. God permits and wills the variegated plurality of viewpoints, insofar as they base themselves on the Christian faith and want to live in it. In this way the most diverse individuals may be touched and find a suitable entryway to faith. The Church tries to formulate dogmatically the chief truths of revelation in such a way that every believer can profess them and so cannot claim that he has no cognitive access to this or that. True, this does not dispense him from having to make his way from his own experience of God to these objective formulations. Naturally, he must not measure dogma by his experience, let alone reduce dogma to it. Nevertheless, it is one of the requirements of his faith that he attempt to find those points of access that correspond to the way in which God has touched him. And anyone who cannot discover them himself ought to have other more experienced people point them out to him. If someone has found good access for himself and has transformed an objectively believed dogma into a subjective and life-giving truth, he can and must do his part to see that through him others likewise grow into the Christian truth.

The source of the Church's dogmas is the revealed word to which Holy Scripture attests. Anyone can draw from Scripture, but he must interpret it according to the Church's understanding of faith and her tradition and, at the same time, constantly understand these as the background and the criterion of dogma. Within this framework he is at liberty to choose the books and words that can guide him personally. But as he chooses, he will understand that he himself has been chosen all along. He will, in the midst of his predilections, enter into an obedience whose ultimate model is the Son's relationship to the Father. To this end there are also various mediating forms in the Church of which he is free to avail himself: this saint rather than that, this order rather than another, and so forth.

c. Knowledge and the Night of the Cross

For the believer, the Son's cry of abandonment on the Cross is perhaps the highest expression of the knowledge of God. At this moment the Son took upon himself the burden of every sin and of all the suffering of the world and thereby completed his mission. He recognizes that what he wanted to do out of love for the Father and for his sake is done. The Son's mission is so perfectly completed that he is bereft of everything. All that remains is his final deed: his night that he was willing to carry through. Insofar as in this night all of the promises and prefigurements of the Old Covenant are fulfilled, this night is the final confirmation of the truth and, by implication, the ultimate and supreme knowledge.

Consequently, whoever wants to follow the Lord will make this night the heart of his existence. He will not arrogantly lay claim to it for himself; rather, he will be present in the humble attitude of the lover who has a right to approach the deepest secret of the Lord. The night is a mystery that belongs to the One on the Cross, while the Mother and the beloved disciple stand under it. Everyone who wants to follow the Lord, today as then, can be granted a share in the mystery of the night only as a disciple of the Cross. This is not merely a matter of theoretical considerations about the way of the Cross; it is a calling to mind where love brought the Lord and where (with participation and distance) the all-enduring love of a Christian leads. Just as the Church accompanies the Lord on his way of suffering, so too does every believer: in the prayer of the liturgy and in personal prayer and contemplation. There will be objective knowledge—this is the way Scripture speaks and the liturgy worships—but subjective knowledge also flows from it. It concerns me, moves me, causes me to draw certain conclusions for my life. This personal form that I give to my piety and my prayer will, as was said, be shaped by the mold of the Church's piety, behind which stands the piety of Scripture. Last of all, it will be grounded in the abandonment of the Son on the Cross. By bearing my sins, the Son made possible my faith and opened a way for me to God.

Once he has recognized this hidden spring of all grace, the Christian will not let the matter stop with prayer. He will long in some way, however inadequate, to do penance in the spirit of discipleship and of love. In so doing, he will not delude himself about bearing Christ's sufferings with him. And yet, in accordance with Paul's words, he will try to fill out the gaps that have been left open for him here and there. All of this will perhaps be more of a symbolic gesture, which, however, he is expected to make.

Beyond prayer and penance his whole attitude and way of thinking must declare that he has acquired a knowledge of God in the mystery of the Cross. This overall attitude has to be at its clearest in the case of a consecrated person living according to a rule, which is nothing but the transposition of the mystery of the Cross into a form of life. Every layman, however, can also devise for himself a suitable form shaped by the Cross. But the form of life that takes shape out of the knowledge of the Cross and Resurrection is never restricted to the believer as if he were the center; rather, it is—like the Cross of Christ itself—open to the world and to all his fellowmen. The fundamental law of this form of life is selfless love of neighbor. The Son carries the Cross, not solely in order to satisfy the Father, but for all men. So, too, the knowledge that is gained under the Cross cannot concern only one's personal salvation; one's fellowman, the Church, and the world all have a central place in the field of vision of every Christian piety. Carmel wants to make atonement for the sin of the world; to be in Carmel while being concerned only about one's own salvation would mean to live outside the rule. By means of the rule, the member of an order remains in closest contact with the sin of the world. It is impossible to strive for contemplative knowledge of God without seeing the world of sinners for whom Christ died and, in so doing, unveiled most profoundly the essence of God. If all Christian knowledge were arranged solely around the concept of God, then there would no longer be any room for the knowledge of creation and of the work of the Son, who is perpetually on his way between the Father and the world and between the world and the Father. It is into this movement that all Christian knowledge has to enter. In our prayer and penance as well as in our attitude in life, we must take care that we constantly stretch ourselves in two directions and, accordingly, also receive nourishment from two directions. Indeed, we must remain in a certain equilibrium that is required, not only for the health of our personality, but more decisively for the tension between God and the world.

Anyone who makes statements about the knowledge of divine things is in a situation similar to that of a religion teacher trying to explain something to little children. He talks about God, but he has to know how to present concepts that are accessible to a child's mind. He must not forget that he is speaking to little ones and that his words need to be understood. His images have to adapt themselves to a child's imagination. After all, this was also the way that Christ talked; he never spoke abstractly of God; rather he spoke in such a way that we, limited as we are, are able to grasp it.

4

The Encounter

a. The First Meeting

Young people receive religious instruction; they also have a particular creed; but for them the matter of religion remains in some respects one "subject" among others, such as foreign languages, the sciences, and so forth. Usually it is the parents who have selected a religion and a denomination for their children, while the children grow up either seeing it as something more or less obvious or being indifferent to it. They do their churchly duties as they do their homework, and they do not have to be more deeply affected by it.

Only when man grows up and begins to plan and shape his life himself, when he chooses among possible careers the one that seems suited to his talents and inclination, can he desire to settle the question of his religion and denomination as well. But he occupies himself at first mainly with the things over with he has control: after all, he has to secure a stable and, if possible, prime position in his professional life; he has to acquire expertise, well-founded opinions, and influential friends. It remains to be seen in all of this whether he thinks he has a similar liberty to arrange religious matters as well or whether he will come up against a limit here and ask himself what arrangements God has in mind for him. At some point, whether it is during Mass or when he is praying or reading or talking with friends, this question can become unavoidable: the traditional picture of God he received growing up suddenly sinks into oblivion, and man encounters God. It may happen as abruptly as when you bump into a passerby on the street: you cannot avoid meeting him, turn into a side street, hide, or look intently at a window display. The two of you have caught each other's eye: whether or not you exchange greetings is another question.

God shows himself; God speaks. He may speak to other people, too, but in any case he is speaking to me. How the person next to me understands his word is none of my concern right now. God has chosen this hour and this occasion to meet me. He has the means and the power to do it in such a way that man cannot dodge the issue but has to make a decision—and will. When the believer realizes what is happening, he is usually so struck that he stands there like someone who has just been wounded. A part of him that before was whole and promised peace and seemed to have a future has broken into pieces and cannot be glued back together again. The familiar country road has suddenly stopped, and he now finds himself before a chaotic thicket. Man's whole helplessness, indeed, his whole lack of future, yawns open—that is, unless he resolves to jump over his own abyss to God. God's "thou" is so surpassingly powerful that man, no matter which way he moves, always remains in his clasp. A truce with God is out of the question. You have to stick it out right where you are until you have heard everything. God does not just go his way; he wants to be listened to now, and man has to be all ears. What God has to say will not take many words; it may be a single word, which afterward can be stretched out into a whole sermon. It is also possible for everything to get stuck in the initial stages so that God has to meet man for days and weeks and years until man gets an inkling of what he is saying. But as man's Creator and Redeemer, God is so close to him and understands him so well that he knows precisely how he has to handle him, how to make himself heard, what word man will respond to without fail.

Much of the above lies in the Lord's words to the disciples: "Follow me." If a man has heard those words, it is up to him to explore how he is meant to take them, how he can respond to them, and where he has to turn for the clarity to settle these questions. He may also have heard less, something like God's saying to him: "Here I am", the meaning of which slowly clarifies itself from the surrounding mists. In some deep recess of his mind he already knew that God was there; it seemed that there was no further need for

any meeting to occur and that all it would take was a
reminder. And yet, when God makes known his presence to an individual, this act has to have a singular,
a deeper significance. And his former awareness of
God's presence may now appear to be a very precar-
ious matter after all; he knew about it as something
held in reserve for possible use later on, which, however, was not for the time being of immediate concern. In the same way a student of Latin learns a lot of
vocabulary that will become meaningful only much
later, when he has to read one of the poets. When
the hour comes for the student to hold his Virgil in
his hands, first his mood is quite solemn. Someone
who understands the text is there, the teacher, who is
willing to help the pupil, who comes prepared with
only a little knowledge. Something analogous happens when man meets God or in the time following
this encounter. Say someone has learned a variety of
things, in catechism class, and so on. Some of it he
has retained; some of it he has consigned to oblivion. Only now do these things suddenly become rel-
evant. Will man, with his prior knowledge, measure
up to the text of God? But the teacher, God himself
or one of his helpers in the Church, will assist us to
read the text correctly. That means, of course, that
one's whole life must be newly ordered and planned.
What was most deeply hidden must be drawn forward
into the light; everything must be examined so that
we know what is useful. God acts thereby with great

regard and at the same time without any regard: the first because he above all shows and proves that he does not want to leave my life without meaning, because he himself chooses the hour and now declares what the order of life should look like. The second, because he clears out everything, old and new. Things that were apparently insignificant suddenly turn out to be important. Things apparently important are made into scrap iron. What was indispensable is carelessly left to the side. What was impossible is now indispensable. Everything is turned upside down simply because I have encountered God, and now the only thing that counts in his word.

For the most part everything happens so suddenly that man attempts some resistance. It cannot possibly be meant so seriously. Most likely there is a milder sense to God's language. Whatever is not achieved today can just as well be done tomorrow or perhaps later. One who is taken by surprise longs for time to think it over and still more time to think it over. Since God has eternity at his disposal, he cannot be suddenly in such a hurry, if, that is, one should happen to come across him . . .

b. The Decision

If God decides to speak and to call someone, he does not, for the most part, take into account the place where the one called finds himself. At the same time, this place no longer appears fixed; the one called sits as though in a train that travels through the countryside with new images constantly appearing. Wherever he looks there is something fascinating; immediately thereafter everything is again different. And yet all of this contributes something essential to the situation of the traveler. Before there was a view of the sea; now there are high mountains, and he should find an answer in himself that corresponds equally to both. He should know something that can be used everywhere. And this something lies simultaneously in God and in man; he simply cannot realize it. He knows for certain that God calls, just as he knows that *he* must give an answer, but his inner situation changes so quickly that his answer never seems to be the right one. There could be—and this is indeed expected—a Yes that is like falling into an abyss. A Yes that appears completely impossible. The air has become so thin that the speaker no longer hears his own voice. And if he said Yes in a life-threatening situation, the landscape has already fully changed again. It is as if God should want the Yes to be the only thing that remains the same, the only thing still standing, while all the rest changes. Man cannot arrange things so that the train stops in order to give him time to orient himself better. If the train were to stop, allowing man to give a reasonable, well-grounded, qualified, and conditional Yes, a Yes that included everything that seemed possible to him (presumably by degrees), then such a Yes would immediately resound in all its emptiness as a mere echo of his own reason. But, someone will object, did not God himself endow man with reason? Indeed he did, but for a moment man's understanding no longer has the decisive word; God himself does. Therefore it does not help to close one's eyes in the desire to forget the passing landscape. It is still there, and it must be thought about together with the answer. Man has to see it and say Yes; however, this view should be characterized as a seeing in God.

Until now the circumstances of life were given and accepted by man almost without question; they were aspects of his existence. Now it is a matter of distancing oneself from these circumstances in order to attain complete freedom in God. As a result, the main areas of life appear to shift. What was insignificant becomes essential, and what appeared decisive for everyday life loses its meaning. In order to be free, man must affirm simultaneously the old and the new situation. Only then does his Yes gain the necessary breadth. He can approach a thousand things from a new angle, and at each approach he can express his Yes more clearly. Of course, he can give a global Yes and fundamentally renounce everything that has gone before. But this total Yes should not be made too precipitously; he should give sufficient thought to each individual item. The same, original Yes should resound at every place and should point toward God without looking back. At the same time, however, this unreserved pointing toward God will contain countless backward glances at what exists in order to prove itself in individual details.

For the believer, this broadening of his Yes is a preliminary stage that allows him to anticipate the future broadening of his faith and the demands of God. He affirms all, and he affirms nothing. And finally, his Yes, naked and, as it were, totally deprived of its strength, goes toward God: without strength, because it cannot be supported by any arguments; and yet in full strength, because it lays claim to man's entire strength—and because it already fully needs and uses this Yes for the coming service. Whoever would like to insert some pauses here, in order purportedly to examine the situation, in order to construct his life stone by stone in light of God's demands, has missed his hour. No one is asking about the construction, about the walls that can support him, but about readiness—even for a collapse. There is an urgency: one cannot return to say goodbye or to bury one's dead father. The in-breaking of eternity into my passing life has an absolute and timeless character. There are no points of comparison; there are no possibilities to assess where one stands or to withdraw in order to deliberate with oneself. Only a person who himself is called by God and sent forth will be able to say a word here. This person, without himself knowing it, can be God's mouthpiece and thus help to form a complete Yes.

For the one called, such a point of intersection between eternity and time is unique. So much so that it strikes him like an immense catastrophe. In this intersection the believer is depersonalized. He observes that the place on earth that he has occupied until now has been left free. Much of what has gone into his day-to-day life has been hollowed out. Only thus is he able to move in this space. He realizes that his life was not determined by his personality, strength of mind, or intelligence; rather it was something for which his personality was intended and designed. He occupied that place himself, for good or for ill, until the moment God calls. And in this call God fills the believer with his spirit and strength. The *negative* image of the believer that has existed until now is replaced by a positive one. And man grasps that only his Yes truly gives him a personality. Henceforth, he knows himself both as an individual intended by God and as one who is penetrated by the anonymity of the children of God. In a new sense, he is one among many in the Church, a member of the communion of saints. He becomes one who is sent, someone for whom the mission is more important than he is himself. Like a newly hatched bird, he now can move in the freedom of a new world that is God's world. He need not be anxious; his place is filled and no longer left free; his Yes has its own strength. He has left his hesitations behind. Certainly he will never fully attain the ideal of holiness that God determined for him. However, he may claim the fullness of grace for the path upon which he is now walking. God has prepared this grace for his chosen children: it is here for him.

5

The Word of God

a. The Infinite in the Finite

When the Son of God became man, he learned to speak our language and to express himself in our words. The word that we use suffices for him to make himself understood and to declare who his Father is. Insofar as he speaks to us, we recognize that he is the Word of the Father and that what the Father has to say to us is said in him. This fact confers upon the Word himself an unexpected breadth. The Word is divine; God himself is the Word. From all eternity the Word abides in the realm of the Father, and he does not cease to be this Word even when he lives among us. His being Word is not only expressed through language; it also lies in his attitude and in his entire divine-human essence. Certainly he expresses divine truths in human sentences—divine truths that are so immense that we can endlessly occupy ourselves and grapple with the fullness of these words. And yet these utterances do not stand there separately; rather, they are always embedded in the Son's entire complex essence. For the words spoken by him remain bound to him as speaker, because only in him do they receive their final meaning and their life. The spoken word maintains its meaning through the centuries, not only because the Son in heaven is just as alive as he was on earth, but also because he never separates himself from his word. It remains in him who is life. It can never become a dead word. However definitive a divine word wishes to be, it remains also a spoken word anchored in the Son. As a result, this definitiveness is at the same time an always new emergence. The anchoring of the word in the Son is an expression of the vitality of the being and will of God, but also of the ever-present coming forth of the Son from the Father and also the Holy Spirit from the Father and the Son. The word is never tired or exhausted, never expelled or banished, but remains bound to the speaker wherever it is sent. It is comparable to the Eucharist, in which the form of bread and wine are inseparable from the Lord's being as long as they last.

When today a word of consolation from the farewell discourse or the Our Father comes alive, this is not the result of an artificial vitality that flows into it from the preacher or the person reading the Scriptures; rather it comes from an eternal and divine vitality that is displayed in its effects. It may be that the person interpreting the Lord's parables draws on other images to convey more clearly the parable's meaning—comparisons and images from our time that never would have occurred to an earlier age and, indeed, would be unintelligible to it. However, the content and meaning of the parable itself and the bridge that it builds between heaven and earth (God's drawing near to man), all of this must remain the same because of the unchanging vitality of the word of God. "The kingdom of heaven is like . . .", begins the Lord, as he takes a small familiar image that everyone can understand. Of course, outside of this context this image would never mediate an idea of the kingdom. In a non-Christian setting, the sprouting of a seed will never give rise to the idea of heaven on earth. In the mouth of the Son, however, this image contains the hope for eternal blessedness. Taken together, all the parables amount to a loosely associated series, but when heard with Christian ears, every image broadens our view of eternal life. Behind every human word stands the word of God, which reveals God's being.

Human eyes take hold of the appearance of the Son of Man. The apostles could tell us much about the way Lord presented himself. For the unbeliever, this appearance could not be distinguished from the behavior of others. However, in his speech and his gestures, Christ mediates grace. Through his entire being the divine streams forth upon men, stirring, awakening, and changing them so that they can grasp why he is the Word.

Not many words of the Lord have been preserved, but there are more than enough to call upon every man and to provoke an answer to God. And before man answers, he must receive the word and allow it to be as it is; he must allow himself to be stretched by God's fullness. Above all he must perceive his claim, his engagement, and the obligations that follow. If this characteristic of the word were recognized, man would be able to experience the extravagance of the word. And even if he were to take in every word and become a carrier of the word, the extravagance nevertheless would spill over beyond him. He can never keep the word entirely sheltered in himself. For he is only an image and mirror vis-à-vis God, and he can never give everything that he has received from God back to God. Even when he somehow has a presentiment of the dimensions of the divine, he cannot leap out of his created realm. There remains the inability to correspond to God, as much in comprehending the truth as in discipleship and in holiness. Every saint runs up against this limit; every disciple and everyone who genuinely prays must meet up with his inability even in those moments when he is not preoccupied with his own concerns, because the word is so strong within him that it graciously, so to say, wipes away his human limitations. The word is so alive that it can carry in itself as living what is dead in the sinner. The little Thérèse "chooses all", but she knows that in the choice of discipleship a limitation nevertheless is imposed upon her. She does not need to worry (although she knows this); the Lord will take over her worries and allow them to dissolve in his grace.

b. Full Correspondence in the Word

As man, the Son must find his way into the fullness
of the word that he himself is. His presence among
men, which becomes a new task day after day, which
must provoke again and again the question of how
he should form the word. When he hears or speaks
words, he has to bring them into relation to the
fullness of his mission, so that they can participate
in this fullness. The word that he speaks must be
understandable to the highest degree as the most valid
expression of his mission that stems from the Father.
He himself is the Word of the Father from all eternity,
and he understands his own unlimited meaning. But
as man, in terms of his human nature, he has to learn
his own eternal word and find the right expression.
He must allow himself to be struck by the word that
he is. He must submit to the word and encounter it
with the esteem due to the word of God. He is "I"
as man and as God, and in this "I" there can be no
discrepancy between them, because as man he is not
a mirror image of his own divine being, but, rather,
he is the active word of the Father, the incarnate, only
begotten Son in the entire depth and uniqueness of
this word.

However, when as God he hears the word that
he speaks on earth, and when he grasps its entire
breadth of meaning, then he places this word in the
midst of his eternal love for the Father, where his love
for man also has its place. He sees how the Father

receives this word, what meaning it has in his love, how it affects things and at the same time how it is integrated into the circulation of divine love. When he speaks the same word to man, he sees that, while the word cannot forsake him, there exists too little love among men for the word to be fully received. It remains, therefore, in a kind of suspension: on the one hand, it exists as his divine word; on the other hand, it is not granted the response of a complete reception. He speaks the word fully, but he only seldom hears an answer. And when one comes, it lacks the power that lay in the word.

Perhaps he feels this dearth of response most deeply when he prays in the desert. There he worships the Father and speaks with him, while mankind is distant and separated by a wall of indifference and alienation. For the Son, the desert is solitude with God. So is the time he spends among men, though, basically it should not be. When the Son turns to men, he has to be able to bring his word together with man's answer back to the Father, with their Yes embedded in his Yes. His voice suffices to shelter each human word and to give these words their final fullness. However, before he gets involved with those who are indifferent, he has already lived together with his *Mother*.

From the moment she gives her Yes to the angel, the Mother knows that she will carry God's Word within herself. She understands somehow that the

Son and the Word of God are one. At the same time, she looks back on the history of Israel, which was a history of the word of God with his people. She knows the promises, and she is permitted to contribute to their fulfillment. She knows the power with which God the Father spoke to the people. She knows how he sent the prophets and through them spoke words that were hardly ever observed and almost always ignored and disregarded. But now the Word has become flesh in her. In her Son the fullness of the Word and human existence are not to be separated. When Mary speaks with the little child who cannot yet talk, she nonetheless knows of the fullness of the Word in him. She takes all the child's gestures—his sleeping and drinking, his smiling and crying, his small movements—as an expression of the Word in his fullness. Her happiness is motherly and at the same time Christian, it is the happiness of a person who has encountered his God. It is complete and pure happiness that knows no gloominess, none of the obstacles that men usually place in the way. God's Word can meet Mary unhindered and place her in full light, for there is no darkness in her. She receives everything as a gift of complete joy and correspondingly rejoices. She also knows that days of worry, concern, sadness, and the sword will come, but these days are not here. It belongs to her obedience to receive joy joyfully.

In the encounter with the child, she is not a student

who sits at the feet of the master; she is a mother who allows herself to be full of delight. She does not conceptually sort her experiences and label them according to various truths of the faith. She discreetly takes her place as a mother within all the other things that are set in relation to the Son. And she fulfills her task with the joy that has been granted to her. If we consider, then, circumstances that she does not understand—such as with the twelve-year-old—her obedience remains intact. She will always answer in exactly the same spiritual disposition that is instilled in her by the Word and the Spirit. She will experience as much anxiety as she is intended to have. In the midst of disquiet, she will react as is expected of her by the Son. In the Mother's disquiet in relation to the twelve-year-old, many things come into view in terms of how Christians are called to respond to anxiety by experiencing and taking to heart the Word of God. One should not desire more than what is granted at the moment; one should remain standing at the place one is shown. Mary neither presumptuously arrogates something to herself, nor does she lapse into quietism. She perseveres in complete obedience and love for the Word; she undertakes her mission exactly as it appears to her today.

When later the apostles encounter the Son and his word calls them, they also will enter into discipleship. But their Yes will never catch up with the Mother's Yes. The apostles feel themselves largely taken unawares. They are full of questions that they do not ask at the moment but that they will later remember. It is as though they set these questions aside or even hid them, keeping the weak places of their faith under lock and key in the face of possible encroachments of the word, which perhaps already now would like to swallow up everything in them in order to make a clean start and bring forth from them an adequate response. But they have not gotten so far. They are limping behind. It belongs to their fate to be always late in relation to the word. Only days later do they understand what basically was intended for the moment. Perhaps there are many things they never fully understand. And yet they are so shaken by grace that they do the most obvious thing in a kind of half-awakened faith.

With Mary the question does not arise as to whether she is half or fully awake. Obedience and love have fully taken hold of her because she has completely given herself away. Perhaps it belongs to the distance of reverence that the apostles respond as they do and in this context pose their questions and uncover their lack of understanding. Thus the word of the Lord shines all the more brightly and shows that, as man, he does not know the weakness of ignorance, forgetfulness, or lack of readiness.

6

Man's Response

a. The Yes Hidden in God

The man who responds to God's word transcends
time. The Lord said: "Heaven and earth will pass
away, but my words will not pass away." When man
responds to this immortal word and knows in faith
that he will be heard, he also knows that his human
word will find its way into the immortal word and
that he will thus leave behind the reality that non-
believers see. The place to which he now goes has,
for the time being, only the characteristics of eternity.
The measures that allow his answer to be received
and considered are eternal measures. The small, hesitant Yes—spoken with inner reservations and sur-
rounded by a thousand questions—gains a portion
of the greatness and inexorability of a world that he
encounters and learns of from the hand of Christ, a
world hitherto unknown to him as an earthly man.

The Yes is the shibboleth that gains him admit-
tance. This entry is definitive. He can advance, im-
possibly, step by step, because the transitory does not
provide a measure for the eternal, and the eternal is

neither a sum of finite moments nor the outcome
of initiations or endeavors. Perfection stands face to
face with one who, till now, was sinful, imperfect,
and frail. By being heard in eternity, the response is
ennobled. The realm that has been prepared for it by
the love of the triune God is the infinite and eternal
realm.

Consequently, one's Yes should not sound hesitant
and flat. In eternity it receives the sound that is due
to the eternal alone. And the one involved sees now
what he has done. He has taken the risk of definitively
breaking free from the security of everyday life, from
the calculations of a dull existence, from the habits
and decay of life, from everything that until now has
shaped his existence and allowed him safely to play a
role that corresponded to his desire for recognition
and peace. He is enabled to break free by a Yes that
he, at first, views as a mere *addendum*. Thanks to his
Yes, he has become homeless and also defenseless.
And yet, he cannot be seized by dizziness as though
plunged into emptiness, for what catches him, surrounds him, forms him, and lifts his spirit is the permanent one, the Word himself. From now on he will
view the world from the perspective of the Word. He
will become aware of the world's transitoriness in a
variety of ways. He will see not only men, cities,
kingdoms, and cultures pass away, but also his own
views and opinions, and much besides. Not in such a

way that he will immediately have to say No to everything, but his former choices will appear uncertain to him. In many areas where until now he spoke only a timid and questioning Yes, it will be necessary to speak a definitive Yes. In many areas where he earlier said Yes, he must now give a clear No. And every kind of self-assurance that has accompanied him until now will be replaced by God's assurance. What until now he thought, decided, and established for himself and others will lose its clarity because the limits of finitude have fallen away. What was reckoned according to time must now be thought about in terms of eternity. However, he stands face to face with eternity as something unknown. For him to think that he has understood something of eternity would appear, today more than ever, a presumption. Eternity can only be understood in light of the Lord. And yet he will now know that with every confession and Communion, with every reception of the sacraments, he is receiving eternity in a new way. The eternity of God strikes something in him that belongs to the mission of every saint and that is given as a possession to him, although he in no way has a claim to it. Indeed he must renounce precisely this possession to preclude anyone from making a connection between it and him. And yet it belongs to him, because he belongs to God and because his response now means everything that God is.

It can also occur to this person that his Yes was not spoken by him. Perhaps God made use of him completely at random, in order to hear out of his human voice the divine Yes. A fantasy of God's, a game that reflects his mood. And yet it is a game inside eternity. As a child, Jesus played with a ball that was full of holes and left lying around unused. Yet as soon as he grabbed hold of it, the holes disappeared and its uselessness was forgotten. God plays in whatever way suits him, and the toy must correspond accordingly. Not through a change that one could bring about through oneself, but rather through the mysterious, though perfect, claim of God himself. It can happen that a preacher says things that he believes are of great importance. Perhaps he even has a specific listener in mind to whom he must say these things in order to bring about his conversion. And then the unexpected happens: he speaks an accidental, perhaps additional word—a word that afterward he does not even remember—and it is this word that is heard and bears fruit.

When we look at it more closely, the Yes that man speaks is not identical with the Yes that God hears and then shows to the one who says Yes in his new condition. Through this Yes, which is sheltered in God, he receives a share in the word of the Lord. Therefore, he no longer knows it as his own.

b. The Transformation of Life

A man encounters the word of Christ and submits
to it. He renounces something that he has wished
for himself and to which he is very attached; he sup-
presses a disordered desire in his spirit; he works tire-
lessly to bring about a new way of thinking. Perhaps
he goes as far as the total self-gift of a life of following
the evangelical counsels. To the extent that he submits, he notices how concrete the word has become
for him. It was a word in Scripture written for all, and
now it is a word of the Lord personally addressed to
him. This word guides him and penetrates his entire
life; it unexpectedly lays claim to many small things
of everyday life, and, at the same time, it determines
the great decisions of life. Before, the word had an
audible ring; from now on it has become a voice that
speaks here and now with this individual. What was
generally and carelessly promised will be specifically
and precisely demanded. The Christian belongs to
God and lives for God. But what does this mean in
the concrete? The Word shows us, and he who submits to him leads a new life—the life of the word.
Because it is life, it is concrete. And because it is
concrete *and* living, it is all pervasive and all pene-
trating. It sets standards that are simply beyond man;
he has to place himself as a whole in the service of
the word. And now he understands that through the

word the right distance between himself and his Lord
has been established. Of course, he knew abstractly
about this distance—like one knows about a wall. In
an exceptional case he could reach this point; perhaps he could go a half step farther and bump up
against the unknown (which the Lord was). Now
the distance means fullness—a visible, palpable, and
living fullness. This fullness has swallowed up the
wall into itself. The distance is now something ben-
eficial, and it can constantly be kept in mind as one
prays and works. The truth, the real nature of the
distance, means so much for the new unity between
the one who says Yes and the Lord that the Lord himself takes responsibility for all that man is not able to
achieve. The reciprocal relation in distance gives rise
to a new communion in the collaboration of the Lord
with the one devoted to him. It follows that man no
longer needs to concern himself with the measure.
He can turn over to the Lord the achievement and
all of its conditions. He does what the word and his
obligation call on him to do. He does this as well
as he can, and he does not need to worry about the
fruitfulness of the rest. This will be brought in, not
on his part, but on that of the other. And so confidence and faith become new, because things that appear unshakable become shaken in an eternal light.
Grace and service are brought into a new relation:
we can no longer fix the boundaries between hand-
ing over and taking over. In this relation the divine

unity of life between Father and Son in the exchange of the Holy Spirit is opened up so that the one who says Yes receives a share in the exchange of absolute love. Because love is eternal exchange, he need not be anxious about his task. It is better for him to love without limit and allow himself to be loved without limit. The strength of his Yes draws its life, in any event, from the strength of the word of the Lord.

If he then returns to Scripture and attempts to grasp the meaning of the words in contemplation, a thousand new possibilities open before him. He can discover the word in him, around him, and everywhere, and he can allow it to become a living word. He is overwhelmed that there is so much light and so much power and that the most insignificant reality, when measured by the eternal, can survive in its presence. He cannot stop marveling, for since he has heard the word, everything has changed in relation to the word's meaning and in light of the responsibility that his Yes has placed on him. In the midst of suffering, hardship, and sighs, he now enjoys something of the beauty of eternal life, in which he participates through the word. The walls of his room have remained the same, also the book in which he is writing and his manual labor. And yet, everything has become different and will be done differently.

He will also get to know fatigue, and for moments, whose duration lies outside his control, he will doubt his activity and what happens to him. And still he knows that the meaning is secure, not in him, but in the living word. He does not see how his insignificant activities enter into the great meaning that lies in God; he remains outwardly the same. All he knows is that everything *is* preserved in the word, which carries all things and thus vouches for all things.

c. Attuned by Christ

Man's first Yes is a gift that spans the distance, as though he threw a ball from time into eternity. God accepts the response that is thrown to him and gives it the necessary form. Through his grace and readiness to listen to man, God bestows on man's word an audibility, fullness, and breadth that confer upon him the *dignity* of a valid response to God's own word. And now man is pulled in the wake of his response. He does not feel it in such a way that he would now grow in his own eyes. He knows, however, that he has been received into holy realms, and this makes a deeper claim on him to attune his thinking and doing to these realms. He turns wholly toward God, which allows him to forget himself more and more. He appears to himself as if nonexistent because God *is* and the world belongs to God. His response must move toward God's being. What he has to do is important, not because he is doing it, but because God asks for it. The levels have shifted. In the participation in God's word that he now receives, not only have the standards of judgment changed, but also the manner of experience. He has always known joy and sorrow, but now they are determined by what brings joy and sorrow to the Lord. The things that influence his feelings have lost the measure of something only human; the measure is no longer centered on his own "I", nor is it immanent to the world. Things are for him as they are for God and his kingdom. Therefore he does not need to shed more tears or laugh more loudly, but in all of his personal feelings he will sense the objectivity of the divine. His experience and his solidarity with others will not be less genuine, but they no longer depend on his personal ideas. On the contrary, it is a part of his new life for him to see everything with which he is interiorly concerned in its proper perspective and in the right light. His ability to discern is not thereby weakened, but the permanent willingness to receive and the freedom of confrontation will allow him to perceive the objectivity that stems from God. Since he looks away from himself, his desire for this objectivity will grow ever greater; not only as a result of his zeal, his longing for divine things, and his love for the triune mystery, but also because of the growth in him of an objective desire for objective truth. God will give him this objectivity with open hands. His life will be too short to work through, even on a superficial level, everything received. He will constantly receive new gifts, and they will make him continually more gifted. He himself will barely perceive the change but will be able to grasp only the increase of that which is given by God. It may happen that it will be too much for him, but even this experience of superabundance can be willed by God. It is a sign that man's response was truly taken into the word; the word does not depend on the response, but it remains divine life. The response is transformed according to his form; it is made serviceable according to his concept of service. The most insignificant things—things forgotten and unrecognized, things for which the Christian did not know he was responsible—can now receive a meaning within the fullness of the word.

Also the sacramental life and prayer are transformed. Communion becomes a joy within the joy of the Lord who communicates himself. Confession becomes a penance within the penance of the Lord on the Cross. Prayer becomes before all else a reception of the self-revealing Lord. Everything receives its assigned place in the divine Word and in the Word becomes reciprocal relation and exchange. The Word himself arranges and directs this exchange and fills it with meaning so that the concepts do not get confused but allow for ever-greater clarity. A brighter light is shed on the relation of one sacrament to another, of one form of prayer to another, and one way of service to another. Everything subjective is placed in a brighter light, and this light stems from eternity.

Light and clarity, however, create new demands,

and the Christian must repeat his Yes ever more truly. Every Yes should surpass each previous Yes in its truthfulness, because the word sinks more deeply into the response; where God gives more, he takes more. Man, however, cannot be lost either in service or prayer; he is being led. God gives him the sense for what he must do. Such guidance is valid especially for a life according to the evangelical counsels. The Christian does not need to ponder how he should obey; he has the image of the Son. Therefore he also does not need to develop a theory about the obedience of the Son. He can see it concretely before his eyes, and he can reenact it in his own life, without thereby forgetting that the Lord is ever greater. Even less does he need to calculate the distance between the perfect obedience of the Lord and his own imperfect obedience. It is exactly by not calculating that he can enter into discipleship, away from man toward the Lord. There is no system of levels that would overcome the difference. With levels, one tends to rest: something has been reached, and one looks backward and forward to determines one's position. On the contrary, the one who is in movement does not calculate, because every second he is somewhere else. Movement is enough for him. God lies always ahead of him, and he knows himself to be underway. Thus he also knows that his response is taken into the Word, and the Word is rich enough to fulfill every response.

7

The State of the World

a. Creation Ordered toward the Son and Hope

The entire world was created by the Father with a view to the Son; the Father who creates thus shows his love for the Son. As it comes forth fresh and new from the hand of God, the world is pure and free. However, Adam misused his freedom and alienated himself from God, and creation was dragged into this estrangement. Mankind struggles for its place between subjective alienation from God and its enduring objective meaning as created for the Son. Even after the appearance of Christ on earth, this conflict remains within man. In fact, now that the demand of God has been revealed, it becomes greater. The Word of God has issued forth; but man does not want to encounter God, because he is afraid that he would have to do what he does not want to do; namely, he would have to decide to conform himself to his original purpose. So he prefers to forego knowledge.

Of course, many evade this only from ignorance or partial knowledge. They have heard that there is a God who has spoken, who presented himself as

a God of Love, but who places great demands on
men. In both respects, this God opens the meaning
of existence beyond finitude. Men shrink back before
such a God. They long for a religion that does not
call into question earthly values and proportions.
Thus there arises a sort of contest between the voice
of man, which grows louder and louder in order
to drown out God, and the voice of God, which
maintains its divine volume. The more man wants
to decide for himself about his destiny, and thus also
about his past and future, the more he falls prey to
the limitations of life on earth, the more everything
becomes smaller for him. He pushes greatness to the
side as absurd. Man would prefer anything rather
than to appear absurd. And if he himself has so little
knowledge of God, those who come after will know
even less.

And yet there are moments, whether he wants
them or not, when he is placed before things beyond his ken and his competence because they seem
to come from another world. He denies them, but
they still suddenly make their presence known. And
because things are created as ordered to the Son of
God, this voice from beyond can also resound from
a thing, an event, an illumination—from something
that is almost nothing but is nonetheless something.
It has meaning as something created for God, and precisely now it seeks to unveil this meaning. It is not
about "God in all things" but rather "all things point-

ing toward God, pointing toward Christ", about all things as signposts. Man truly needs countless signposts in order to recognize the path, indeed, even to suspect that the path leads in this direction. And yet it is a path that determines the world. It is, however, directed against the state of the world as the active is against the passive, as life is against death, as obedience and love are against abuse and guilt. The ordering of all things to the Son is a powerful and permanent reality that cannot be denied. It can appear hard, sharp-edged, and merciless. Man must reconcile himself to its unalterability; he cannot break this boulder. It is the primary rock of earthly existence, indeed, of the creative power of God. The path of obedience was traced even before man appeared in the world. There are countless points of entry to this path.

Man, however, has become accustomed to look at the things of the world with the eyes of memory and to judge them according to their past instead of creatively looking at their future and considering them in view of their purpose. So his spirit loses contact with the creative act of God. He works with the stuff of the past, which is, as such, rigid and unalterable, perhaps already putrefied. He must learn to meet God and to work where the creative act takes place: toward the purpose of things, into the future, into hope. The hopelessness of the world's condition lies in the fact that memory has taken the place of creativity and that freedom is placed *behind* man because he does not want to see it *in front* of him. In this way man, while remaining in sin, has reversed the sign of time. In place of the future, he has substituted the past. In God, however, these signs remain unchangeable, and the believer need only adhere to time as it is in God in order to find a way to God in things. It is a path away from the "I" into the future, from hopelessness into expectation, from decay to new life.

If man begins to think about his goal, then he changes the position of the world as he changes his own position. It is as if he were to go back thousands of years in order to get from a gloomy prison into fresh air, to get to the place where God the Father strolls in paradise, the place where the Cross stands and where resurrection and redemption take place. The Father created everything for the Son; in redeeming the world, the Son directed everything anew toward the Father; the circulation of love is guaranteed by the Holy Spirit and made knowable and accessible to us in faith. This occurs without any regard for the condition of the world. Each of us, before we seriously encounter God and recognize the direction of things, lives in the condition of the world. But conversion does not mean turning to God in such a way that one turns one's back on the world. For we are in the world, and we are created as part of the world. When we change directions, something in the world changes. At the moment when we encounter God, we cannot forget the destiny of all others. The Lord emphasized our belonging together in the command to love our neighbor. Our neighbor, however, is the entire world. We have to take the world with us on our personal way to God. Certainly, no one (even were he Francis Xavier) will be able to convert all his brethren in the world. But he will bring the world with him in the spirit of the Carmelite mission so that the world, too, will be able to encounter God. He will take it with him into all of the activities of everyday life. Above all, however, he will take the world with him into prayer, where the final encounter with God occurs. Here the direction of all things is perfectly clarified; here also purity still exists, and from the purity of the divine exchange of love the world can be healed. The world as a whole, as the sum of all the individuals who come from the hands of the Father in the unity of their end, and who, through the hands of the Son, will be given back to the Father in the Spirit. This world is simultaneously created and recreated—recreated because the work of redemption is based on the Resurrection. The old hope of things, the old promise of creation, is fulfilled miraculously in that the world passes through the hands of the triune God.

b. Taking the World to God

When man begins to think, he envisions his adult life in a certain way. He would like to do this kind of work, to have this kind of home, to use his freedom in such and such a way. His plans occupy a great part of his thinking. He tries to gather, to enjoy, and above all to select from his education, his experiences, and comparisons all that the years of youth have to offer. He does this in such a way that everything is ordered to the image of the future that he has designed for himself.

If he is a believer from childhood, his faith will also influence his plans. However, it is seldom that he is aware already in his youth that he has been created by God for a definite purpose and that he has to accomplish something that may indeed lie outside of his human plans but that lies soundly within the divine plan. Once it occurs to him that he is answerable to God, who created him, a confrontation between his own plans and the plans of God becomes unavoidable. This gives rise to areas of friction. If faith is alive in him, the moment will come when he lets his own project fall away in favor of God's plan in order one day to be able to answer God face to face. But even when he does this, he must still reckon with the world that surrounds him, with its immense fullness and variety, its fallen condition and longing for redemption, its moving away from God together with its wish, nevertheless, to find God. He stands in the midst of this world; both realities must be measured, and it is not easy for them to get along. The reality of the world cannot deny the reality of the man standing here; and this man in his singularity cannot dispute the plurality of the world. His self-gift to God must acknowledge the world created by God, if not as a presupposition, then as background. He must take the sinful world along with him, taking note of the world with its progress and its movement backward, its provisions and efforts. Man will not reach his goal without affirming what exists in such a way that he knows therein also the No of distance, fear, and disgust. His Yes is such that it passes through the world to God. The desert or monastic solitude can be the world for him, and his collaboration with the world can be limited to vicarious prayer and atonement: the world is nonetheless present. This presence also bears the stamp of the present moment of history in which each of us is situated. That the world exists would remain true even if the condition of the world were to consist of sheer lies and resisted every Christian intervention. In the truth of its existence, the world still points immediately to God's hand. It may be that this truth urgently points to the untruths of the world's condition, to false problems and situations, to the dangers provoked by human thinking, to the problems raised by technology and its future, which are becoming ever more important for the world, which cannot afford not to work toward a solution. The Christian, who in prayer has the greater world of God's love before his eyes, still must learn to recognize God in this condition of the world. He must look through all the veils and all the lies to see the single truth. Indeed, he must know that the one who prays in solitude with closed eyes and given over to God will experience God no more and no less than he would in the tasks that the world places before him. God may have wanted him in the monastery cell, but he can also place him in the busyness of the technical world of work. He may want to encounter him here and not there, or perhaps there as well as here. The life in a monk's cell is not anachronistic; in the same way, the God-given vocation to live in the world is not a new invention. God can lead someone into the solitude of the mountains in order to be worshipped there by him. He can also place him in a factory or in the chaos of a big-city firm together with countless nameless individuals. If God dares to bring man into such contrary positions, it is because he, as omnipresent, can meet him anywhere. In order not to narrow his image of God or constantly to paint God in his own image, man has to see and recognize the triune God's unforeseeable possibilities and ways of appearing. This knowledge has value, however, only if it allows itself to be integrated in relation to the goal of the world and human life, only if it makes man more capable of meeting

God in the way he has become visible to us in Christ. God speaks to us; we need only find the place where we are able to hear his voice. God addresses his word to us personally; indeed, he addresses himself personally as word to us. But when we hear him personally, we must take care that our contemporaries also hear the word. This is best guaranteed when our attitude testifies that we have heard and that we find ourselves on the way that leads directly to God.

c. The Church in the World

The words of Christ appear to the world as a paradox; his commandments contradict what people consider to be clever and useful. What these words promise is always heavenly; it comes from heaven and leads to heaven. What people do in sin and unbelief, on the contrary, leads to eternal damnation. Heaven and hell are always the ultimate alternatives, and every conversation between God and the still unconverted sinner is thus concerned with setting these two extremes into relief.

The Lord, however, did not throw his word against the unbelieving world unprotected. He founded his *Church* in the midst of the world. The Church has one side open toward the world. Indeed, she herself is the open door for the world, so that the world can enter into God's Holy of Holies, where the mystery of bread and wine is celebrated. Around this mystery the Church is a way of believing and hoping and loving and working whose origin is heavenly. By entering and experiencing this mystery, man finds heaven. And God did not build his Church in such a way that she would be accessible to only a few select souls who live in the purity of faith. He built her as a communal, public place, right next to the street where everyone passes by and can enter when he wishes. Outside is the denial of everything eternal; inside is the receiving into the infinite God of everything transitory in the world. The Eucharist is the innermost event whereby the Church renews herself and makes herself known. But also every divine service, all the remaining sacraments, are encounters with the Lord who gives himself, who points toward his redemptive suffering, and who sends forth those who belong to him endowed with the Holy Spirit. They are called to proclaim the gospel outside and convert sinners. Thus the Church is always a place of encounter between the Lord and the sinner, between heavenly grace and the world. And because it is God who reveals himself in this place, this event is overwhelming and beyond all expectations.

The Church is nonetheless also a worldly reality, a gathering place for Christians that is visible also to others and that serves as a reminder to them. At Mass, in hearing the word and in praying together, Christians themselves are reminded that they are called to be a reminder in the world. They have to show what they have received; they have to bring out into the open the hidden mystery that lives within them. Continually, day after day, they must actualize in visible discipleship the once-only call that they have received from the Lord. The once-only and the multiple are reciprocally related and flow into one another. Indeed, in the man he meets, the Lord sees not only a sinner who will receive absolution, but also a brother whom he receives into his communion of life. In this way he also enabled the word that he spoke only one time on earth to be expanded into a perpetual and living validity. His word lives because Christ lives and because he does not cease to speak the once-uttered word anew and with the same precision it had then. His words appear time-bound to us because we understand them in time. Our understanding, however, is made possible through their connection to eternity.

We are struck and wounded by the word. We could not live apart from the word anymore even if we wanted to. We entered into the Church as nuts with a hard shell; the word broke open the shell. Now, without the shell, we are simultaneously more sensitive and less sensitive: more sensitive because we recognize the traces of the word everywhere and we can no longer live in naive worldliness; less sensitive because the allure of sin does not grab us as much anymore. It is not that it has become weaker, but that it holds less interest for us and God's defense against sin penetrates all the way through us. At every encounter, God also gives us something to remember him, a gift, never something dead, but his living word.

We hear this word in the Church; we find it in undiminished vitality also at home whenever we open the Scriptures or when we return to the word in prayer. Prayer becomes an encounter with the Lord whose word we are permitted to hear without ceasing. We are personally addressed, and we are allowed to respond personally, and in this twofold personal contact, the word works on man until the true ecclesial man takes shape. With every new encounter, God continues to do his redemptive work on that which the Creator declared good at the beginning and for which the Son offered himself on the Cross, not only until we are brought to completion in ourselves, but until we become useful instruments in God's hands for his work throughout the entire world. God's workshop is his Church.

In the Church, as experienced by priests or laymen, there is much that is unchangeable, and this occasionally goes against our spirit of modernization. If we attempt to see and understand with the eyes of love, then we discover that what is unchangeable in the Church comes from the word and its being beyond time. We come to see that, if the distance between the word and us has grown so great, then it is our fault. The word's ultimate meaning remains veiled for us because of our sins and our lethargy. Only seldom are we able to see what is eternally valid in the word. Of course, a perfect hearing and understanding of the word could almost be compared to the beatific vision. Total understanding, as the fulfillment (to the extent possible) of our reason by the meaning of the word, is reserved for eternity. Nevertheless, when we encounter God and fix our eyes on the eternal, we understand from the triune God and the mystery of the Church all that is necessary for us to remain in a living faith and to embody in our lives what we have received from the encounter. We are given what is necessary in order to concentrate in our Yes to the vitality of today's Church not only what *we* need, but also what is needed by our contemporaries for an encounter with God.

8

Work

a. The Christian Meaning of Work

God imposed work as a punishment when he expelled man from paradise. By the sweat of his face shall he till the earth, which brings forth thorns and thistles. Only in the context of this alienation of man as well as nature from God does the character of work as punishment become clear. Even in the Old Covenant, work (even, for example, priestly work) was marked by this distance from God. Work receives a new meaning only through the Incarnation of God in Christ; man's distance from God changes. Insofar as the Son becomes God's worker, both man's work and the objects of man's work (and this includes intellectual work) immediately move toward God. Everything that came from the Father was included by the Son in his plan of salvation, and from here it is given a new meaning: the meaning of redemption.

The life of the Lord is a unified whole: from the manual work of his youth, to the difficult work of his public ministry, to the still more difficult way of the Cross that leads to Resurrection and Ascension. Everything is a single, visible return of man to

God, in which the Son of Man brings us human beings to his own divinity, to the Father and the Holy Spirit. Nothing of what Christ accomplishes is separated from us; he carries us along, and so we go with him. Christian work attempts consciously to bring this movement to completion. Whatever work man does, he can do it for God. With every endeavor, with the most insignificant efforts, man can be certain that God receives the work of his hands and his spirit. Work is never in vain, because no movement toward God was ever for nothing. Work has an eternal meaning conferred by the Resurrection and Ascension.

When Christ died, he left behind few Christians. He planted a seed in the earth whose yield remained practically invisible. If we compare the divinity of his being, words, and deeds with what he achieved on earth, it would seem most appropriate to speak of futility. And yet he loved all unto death on the Cross to atone for our sins. This love remains inseparable from the love that leads him back to the Father. He loved all in the unity of divine love, the greatest that exists. The few disciples are like a visible pledge given to him by the Father. In this the Son knows that the Father has given him all. Every one of these is a worker, and, ultimately, each works in his own way, patiently or impatiently following the directions of the Father, who assigns work to man.

From the perspective of the world, man cannot say

whether work has essentially changed the condition of the earth or whether above all it has become a threat for him. However, it certainly has fulfilled its meaning as punishment *and* as a way to go together with the suffering Son to the Father. What becomes visible does so in faith: it is a way that offers a promise to be fulfilled; it is also a punishment that leads to absolution as the sign of an infinite confession received in grace. Through work man confesses his distance from God, his first sin (which is never simply left behind him), and also every actual sin. However, human work will never attain that radiant character that is possessed and conferred by the sacrament of reconciliation. Human work remains at the highest level fragmentary. It might seem daring to compare work to a sacrament. A sacrament is a pure invention of divine love and its eternal, mysterious fullness. By contrast, behind every work lurks sin. This is seen in the fact that the worker remains a sinner even when the meaning of his work is directed toward grace. All of man's failures pass through the middle of his work. It is seldom that one allows something of grace to shine through one's work: for example, in a painting or a piece of music in which we see or hear only the rejoicing of joy, instead of sighs of exhaustion, doubts, and troubles.

The Church, too, works as an institution. Confession occurs in the Church, which is "work" for both the sinner who confesses and the presiding priest.

Work occurs throughout the entire structure of the
Church where the word is proclaimed and the sacraments are distributed. Also the work of keeping God's
commandments occurs in the Church. We should
love God and neighbor, and this love is work. It is
work sanctioned by the triune God in such a way
that its character as punishment is constantly over-
shadowed by its character as grace. In countless places
the seeds of work are sown, and their fruit is divine
love. Work is practically only a form, and the content
is a love that is always given by God. When a priest
or anyone genuinely builds up the Church or works
on her foundations, he does not see the work of his
hands, for the fruit opens up beyond the visible world
in the kingdom of heaven. He works for the kingdom, whose seed he attempts to sink into the earth
with his last strength. Of course, not everyone who
works on earth can know the final meaning of his endeavors. But the Church knows it, because she, who
is so close to God, hears something of his secret. As
institution, she knows the final meaning of work: the
individuals who live in the Church know this within
the heavenly communion of saints; while those in
the earthly Church still suffer it. One who works
on earth and who, through the sacraments, hiddenly
shares in the fulfillment is only seldom struck by a
ray of grace that would illuminate something of the
meaning of his work. It is as if a wanderer were to
step for a moment out of the shadows into the sun
in order then to continue on his way in the shadows.

Work *is* the shadow, but in a place where at any moment a warm ray from the sun can break in—and here and there it does break through.

Whoever chooses a vocation (even if it were the vocation of perfect discipleship) and is qualified and resolved to pronounce his Yes can do so only to the extent that he submits to the basic law of having to work. Therein he can experience the joy of achievement; he can make the exhilarating discovery that all worldly things are created as ordered to the Son. Still, he cannot escape the drudgery of original sin. He must walk toward the Cross and thankfully gather all of the pieces of the Cross given to him by the Lord.

Faith in God and love for him are such sublime things that man is never done with them. Whenever he thinks he has walked through a room, a new door opens up and shows that he was only in an entryway. There is no end. This endlessness should not weigh man down. It is meant to be an honor, because God himself, who is ever greater, unveils himself to man. And man, who is led into this mystery, must always understand what is shown to him in order to be able to see the ever-greater God beyond it. God wants to pull man after him, and, indeed, he wants to include as well everything that occupies him, his greatest as well as his smallest work.

When someone plans to do something truly great, he knows that his life will not be long enough to fulfill this task. However, if he plans something smaller, something that appears to him more reasonable, the work will permanently carry *his* measure, and, because of his limitations, it will not satisfy. The limits that he sets himself will fall back on him as a burden. Only when he goes beyond his intention to accomplish something satisfying in an earthly way and opens himself to God can the meaning of his work open up for him. It is work within the ever-greater God, and its measure and goal, as well as its limits, are determined by God. And if God himself cares for human work, then he does this as God. In his infinity he lowers himself to encounter man; and thus man, with his plans and work, is raised up into the divine love. What appeared to man in his earthly work to have a certain greatness only now becomes something truly great. For it rests in God, and God bestows his attention on human work, a gift that work, in its transitoriness, could never have expected.

This hesitation means respect. One without respect lays out his own measures and traverses them with his own proud step. However, the one who is respectful and loving bows before the mystery of God and entrusts his plans and their realization to him. And God brings everything into a unity, into the harmony between the harvest of the world and his divine being that only God can establish. When God the Father sends forth his Son so that the Son can accomplish a work with his own hands, the Father does not cast him out of the unity; rather, he sends him from the unity of the triune God back *into* this unity. Jesus' carpentry belongs to God. When Jesus resolves that he will finish shaping this beam today and tomorrow fix this tool, then this occurs within the divine order. He knows that the Father counts on it and needs it for his plans. The Father knows the worker as well as he knows the wood. That is why everyone can carry out his work following after the Son, indeed, alongside the Son, in order to let the Son incorporate him into the work of the triune God. The final meaning rests in God, and the greatness of human activity rests in its being directed toward God. Because man is the image of God, he may do all of his work for Christ's sake and together with him. Thus he confers on his work the radiance of eternity that comes from faith. The trivial work of the day, endlessly fragmented and never finished, receives a complete and unified meaning in God. The beginning and the end lie therein. In this way, time will be gathered into God, and the transitory time of work will be gathered into the meaning of eternal time. Everything that counts and is counted, and everything that measures and is measured, has some share in the imperishable. If someone fundamentally does not want to work, he loses an essential access to eternity. He refuses a form of following Christ and unification with God. If he works as a believer, as someone who submits himself to God by allowing God finally to dispose of his achievements, then his work becomes an expression of his faith and love, and God will not disappoint his hope.

b. Work as Atonement in Christ

God's creating the world as ordered to the Son opens two aspects: first, that the world is *created*, which means it is a work of God. Secondly, it is created with a *purpose*, namely, to give all things to the Son. Naturally, God's activity is undivided, but our praying contemplation is allowed to distinguish these two aspects: the action and the action's direction *toward* something. Furthermore, it is essential for us that God did this work before he imposed work as a punishment. Even in resting on the seventh day, his work is clearly characterized as such. It is meaningful as action and even more as purpose.

After the fall, when man again attempts to order his work to God, he can gain courage and strength from God's creation of the world—God is his model —and perhaps still more from the Father's intention to give away his work. The Father does not harvest the fruit for himself; rather, he leaves it for the Son. Likewise, man creates a work that goes beyond him and that is finally destined, not for him, but for the kingdom of God.

From the beginning, work describes a curve, and it passes through a cycle whose measure lies in eternity. When God placed man in the world, he already gave him a relation to eternity insofar as he created man with a view to the Son. Human work that is insignificant or that is limited to a purely earthly aim, and thus withdrawn from the great circulation of the divine purpose, would have to be characterized, not as atonement, but as sin. It would be activity in disobedience that, estranged as it is from its final purpose, is thus robbed of its fulfillment and final meaning.

When God the Father expelled the first humans from paradise, he already had his eyes on the future redemption in the Son. From God's perspective, the yoke of work that was laid upon the sinners was already a way to the Son. A way of repentance. It was also, of course, a way to confession, because the Son will institute confession at the destination of the path, but also because work in itself contains an automatic confession of the sinner. He must accept the consequences of his original sin in order to attain what God has destined for him. However imperfect this confession may be, it contains traces of the insight that God wants to discover in us: as we carry out our work, he sees that we have accepted our punishment, and thus we are somehow on the way back to him.

And because work has an absolute meaning, everything man does can be brought into relation with this work. His conversation with God in prayer and everything done in the spirit of prayer are finally also a submission to the law of punishment and thus an opening to the law of grace. A monk in a contemplative order experiences in a very distinct way how the hours of prayer, for example, the Divine Office, fall under the law of work. In the same way, a pastor understands how the hours spent in the confessional or spiritual direction are hard work. Prayer tires out the one who prays; he carries its burden. It is clear to him that this work means atonement. In this way, every believer, no matter what work he does, shares in the obedience of a monk or pastor by carrying the burden of work in the spirit of prayer. In faith, each form of work is pertinent to and fits with every other form. In the first place, this applies to work of the same occupation or trade, then to all of the groups among themselves. They all belong to the same circulation of work, and they carry perhaps more than appears to be the case when they are considered individually. And because spoken prayer also belongs to work, some dimension of unspoken prayer lies in every work undertaken in faith. Taken together, the whole forms the work of atonement for guilty mankind, who is on the way to the Son and who has already been redeemed by the Son.

9

The Unmeasurable

a. The Measure of Man and the Unmeasurable

Work forces man to use measurements. He works eight hours a day, and for this work a certain average result is expected from him. The number of a certain kind of item a worker is able to make in a day, week, or year is fixed. Also fixed is the amount he needs to support himself and his family (if a loaf of bread or a dozen eggs cost such and such . . .) and the amount he needs for pleasure (the cost of a ticket to the movies or to a soccer match). His entire existence is saturated with numbers, and each presents a certain measure. When something in the mechanism breaks down, he stands there helpless. For the most part, it has an unpleasant effect. When as a worker he imagines the work schedule of his superior, he sees that he has more holidays, a higher salary, and therefore different pleasures. The superior, however, does not organize his time with any less precision, since he probably also has more work to do and greater responsibility.

If a man gets completely accustomed to the idea that everything can be measured, then he loses any

sense for eternity. His horizon does not reach farther than the measurable, passing time, and mortal
existence. Everything he measures constantly brings
him to limits: there lies the point where what he has
planned comes to an end; beyond it begins something
else to measure. The life of an individual passes away
between such ends and new beginnings. He gets on
top of what he has measured; it has been incorporated
within the compass of his life. He is ruled by the law
of numbers, and he in turn rules over it. The measurements are handed over to him already complete,
and yet he preserves a small amount of freedom in
relation to them. He can compare things (for example, the price of milk); he can also save; he can give
up things that he would have a right to in order to
enjoy others. He accustoms himself to this freedom
in the midst of measurements as though behind bars.

This also influences his thinking. He thinks within
fixed categories that have become so natural to him
that he hardly ever questions them. On the contrary,
he simplifies them more and more.

However, if he meets someone who lives from
faith, he encounters in him God himself. Something
adventurous breaks into his limited existence. He
does not know whether he is thereby weighed and
measured. One thing, however, is certain: his measurements do not suffice to determine these dimensions. His conventional categories, time schedules,
and simplifications cannot cope with the phenome-

non. He had arranged a plan for himself that would allow him to advance in his job in order to be able to afford certain things when he reached the age of fifty or sixty. If the Christian truth is valid, God could frustrate all his plans; he could perhaps even require him to give up his position. In any event, God could demand from him his advance calculations and small arrangements, which now appear to him as countless reservations against God. Who could place conditions on God? This belongs to the most difficult aspects of faith: to let go of the narrow boundaries and divisions we have worked hard to put in place. We must give them up when we encounter the limitless and unmeasurable. Even time can no longer be measured by years and months, but only in terms of the entirety of a life—and the length of a life is unknown. Everything that was measured according to one's own advantage must now be held in contempt. God offers no measures that man could get used to or for which he could use his own system of calculation. The prescribed time for prayer, the commandments of the Church, and the demands of loving one's neighbor strike him as hard, and he does not know how to cope with it. On the surface, the circumstances remain the same: time remains time. Interiorly, however, everything has completely changed: time is now something in which eternity wants to find a place; and measure is now something in which the unmeasurable must be sheltered. Thus everything becomes quite uncomfortable. That which until now was correct is no longer correct, and it is not clear what can serve as a substitute. In many parables Christ speaks about things that are familiar to us: for example, about a heavenly meal, about the true shepherd and his sheepfold, about the lost coin, and about the fig tree that bears no fruit out of season. These things that are known, which man perhaps could learn about with effort, acquire in the Lord's mouth a new and disconcerting taste. Human understanding is brought to an unusual place and bent down before the eternal so that the eternal can become graspable to mortal men. There is also, however, speech about the eternal itself: about the Father's kingdom, about the relation between the Father, Son, and Spirit, and about inaccessible things that nevertheless have a decisive value in faith. Until now, man was accustomed to things having their proper place with a nicely arranged beginning and end. Now things are supposed to surrender both their beginning and end; their meaning should be extended into eternity beyond the reach of our understanding. If man discovers himself in a word of God and notices how the measures slip from his hands, he becomes dizzy. He still knows what *was* the case up to now; however, what *will be* in the future has almost no common measure with the past. The standard of his reason no longer provides a valid measure; instead, it is provided by the immensity of God that wants to find precisely in this small human life a place and foothold in the world. A tree in a flowerpot. The hardest thing required of the believer is to place himself at the disposal of something incomprehensible, something that begins to make sense only through love. Until now he was collecting, gathering, counting, and disposing; now he is meant to open himself in such a way that the hands he holds out to collect have to remain apart. He is embraced by God in such a way that he is no longer capable of embracing anything. He must keep himself as vessel, and he cannot guarantee what this vessel will contain. He no longer knows it because he must allow what he had once well protected and thought through many times over simply to flow into the infinite, according to a rhythm that God alone determines.

b. The Unmeasurable and Obedience

When Mary flees to Egypt with the infant, she follows a directive from Joseph, who himself had been ordered to flee. The perfectly supernatural character of this flight opens heaven: if Joseph had to explain why he undertook this flight, he could only say that it had become clear to him that God wants it this way. However, he has no measurement by which to examine this certainty. Mary follows without questioning. He bears responsibility for her, and she submits to him. However, she does not follow him on the basis of natural reasons alone; she also follows because this is included in the Yes she gave to the angel. The fact that everything she will have to do is always already included in her Yes takes away the measuring of her days. She must always allow the things of today to be mirrored in the eternal instructions. She lives a hidden life on earth that constantly unfolds in the public openness of heaven. She knows that she is watched from heaven and that her Yes is perpetual.

It is a flight from home to escape danger. This flight is, however, a movement into an ever-greater obedience, which keeps apparently everything open, especially for the child. The child is still too young; the responsibility lies with the adults. Nevertheless, Mary's Yes passes through the Son, for *he* has always already given his eternal Yes to the Father to redeem the world. When later the cup is offered to him at the Mount of Olives, and he receives it, he immediately assumes responsibility for his own Yes—as a man before men and as God before the Father and the Spirit. And yet he includes in himself the Yes of his Mother, which has not faded away. And this responsibility for the world that he carries (and that goes back to the responsibility for him once carried by his Mother and Saint Joseph) lacks any kind of measure of which he could gain an overview and control.

At times this measure can appear as a lightning bolt: it was shown to Joseph in a dream; Jesus knows the task of the Cross. Of the Son's eternal movement toward the Father, small fragments can be seen, in which the measure and the responsibility can be read, but they are always embedded in that which is un-measurable. We can perceive this in light of the excess of obedience, which we continue to see as a kind of measure (even though it surpasses our measure). In the encounter with God, if a man answers with a Yes whereby he surrenders his whole life and his whole obedience to God, he must, in order to know what he is doing, hold on to that aspect of the Lord's life that reminds him of a measure. As Saint Ignatius shows in his spiritual exercises, he always chooses a greater disgrace and humiliation. If it is pleasing to the Lord so to lead him, man chooses a path marked by the Lord's Cross. He chooses the path of the flight to Egypt, or wherever it may be, in order to leave a "here" that he can no longer hold onto. He chooses expropriation. But he does so in the first place on the basis of a certain measure, which is revealed in the Lord's life. He knows that behind this life the entire unmeasurable triune life of God lies hidden. He knows that God lowered himself in encounter-ing man (which is always connected with the gospel) in order to present him with things characterized by measure so that man would not lose his bearings but could accept in obedience that which God shows him.

It may happen that man, in the moment of his encounter with God, would know exactly what he should sacrifice. He could imagine his today and his yesterday, also the previous months and the past year, even his whole life up to now. He could allow all of this to come back to life before his eyes in individual events in order to measure approximately what he would lose if he surrendered it to God. He would measure according to the past and according to its significance. If, however, a Yes is pronounced in a Christian way and in humility without man making himself important and measuring himself, nothing from his future can be foreseen. At most he can assess what the Lord showed to him though his life as the Redeemer. Man knows that an ever-greater grace lies hidden for him therein, but he has no measure for this "ever greater". He has to die to himself. If he does that, he reaches with his Yes into eternity. He tastes already now something of that which he will taste at his death when he stands face to face with eternity. Everything that comes from the beyond and that God offers is unmeasurable.

If, however, after he has pronounced his Yes, he reintroduces his own measures; he robs himself of access to the eternal on earth. A member of a religious order who would like to live according to the measure of today and plan and calculate on the basis of today everything that still lies before him would die by a false death. He would have entered into a no-man's land, for he would no longer belong to the living of this world, but nor would he belong to the eternal life that opens to him through a measure-less obedience. He can no longer use worldly measures, but at the same time he also robs himself of the unmeasurableness of that which is eternal, because he has decided not to rest in God's hands without worries like the lilies in the field. Thus he has fallen into something unreal and untrue. The earthly measure can contain small truths and the unmeasurableness of the Yes opens the ever-greater truth of God; there is no third between these two.

c. Measure and Unmeasurableness in Ecclesial States

To live in the unmeasurable and from the unmeasurable does not mean living in disorder. It means receiving today's order as an order—as an order, however, that lies beyond our understanding completely in God and whose measure is the absoluteness of eternity. And yet, as order, it is a knowable measure for us. The one who gives to God his entire future with its promises and entrusts to God the order of his life through the choice of the evangelical counsels binds himself to an ecclesial rule. As a form of life through which the Holy Spirit blows, the rule mediates between the measure of ordinary Christians in the world and the unmeasurable reality that lies in a pure Yes. This mediation is not a compromise; rather, it is a way that heaven draws close to earth. It is a continuation of the way that the promises of the Old Covenant are fulfilled in the New Covenant and the way that the Son of Man bends down to the one who gives himself to Christ.

If we look closely at the rule of an order that has been approved by the Church, we are perhaps astonished to find two things bound together: an almost pedantic precision that takes into consideration every possible situation and the wholly uncompromising character of faithfulness to the vows. It is as if the unmeasurableness of the Yes must help that which is measured, so that man, who bound himself with his Yes, does not lose sight of what he has to surrender, but unceasingly discovers again, in every detail measured by the given order, new points of access to the unmeasurableness of God.

The Christian in the world and in a parish who does not live according to such a rule should by all means know something of the unmeasurableness of life bound to a rule. The fact that he has chosen another path for himself does not exempt him from the duty to know what is more greatly ordered and perfectly given over. This knowledge should not paralyze him, because he should be able to gain from this image certain insights for his own life. In living together with a wife and children, much will be imposed on him that requires a radical attitude of sacrifice; he will often feel the touch of the transcendent. He cannot limit the scope of the "rule" to his

family, but he also has to include his broader surroundings, his work as well as society. God rouses
him, as it were, by providing an irreducibly twofold
measure of his duties—like the Christian duty of love
of neighbor: he must carry them out in relation to the
inner circle of his family and in relation to the outer
circle of his surroundings. He cannot limit his self-
gift and love of neighbor to his family. That would
be a form of egoism. He himself would thereby determine the measure of Christian love and thus refuse
its unmeasurableness. In the same way, he cannot do
the contrary and seek to meet his neighbor only in
the outside world. In not having the measure at his
command, although it nevertheless still obliges him,
he experiences something of the unmeasurableness
of God.

If a Christian in the world encounters a true member of a religious order and comes to understand
his rule, his way of thinking, and his way of life,
a breeze of eternal life blows over him from here.
He will understand something of the unmeasurableness of Christian life, and this knowledge will confer new dimensions to his measured life. A lively exchange of Christian ways of life is fruitful. Indeed,
this exchange could be understood as an image of the
inner divine exchange of love. The religious did not
enter his order to escape from the world but in order
to serve the world in God. But also the layman in
the world is called to perform a divine service that

is entrusted to him. He can only recognize the extent of this service if he knows what occurs in religious life. Moreover, he must always submit anew his measure to the unmeasurable and allow himself to be determined and transformed by it. The dangers of the unmeasurable and the dangers of the imposed measure seem at first contrary, and yet, seen more deeply, they are the same: man constantly tries to determine himself. However, just as the Christian must be open to the unmeasurable in order to recognize his Christian measure, so the one who lives in the world of the vows must know about the small measure that is imposed on his brother outside. This exchange is important for both of them. Something that takes place in the triune exchange should also be present on earth among the Christian forms of life. These two not only communicate in Christ's Church, but they are also animated by the thought that creation as a whole is created for Christ.

10

Joy

a. The Predominance of Joy

God can encounter man in the light of his glory in such a way that it changes man's whole life. His faith begins to radiate so that everything around him is lit up by it. Everything is given a new purpose; what was uncertain until now becomes clear to him and to those around him. This illumination is joy, a participation in the communal joy.

The Son is the Father's joy, perfect divine joy. He lives for the Father, and everything that belongs to the Father is his. He has a complete share in the possessions of the Father and, therefore, also in his joy. He also shares in everything that is directed against the Father, which then hurts him and moves him to redeem the world. He redeems it in the joy of the Father and in order to increase the Father's joy, but also in his own joy—the joy of giving a gift to the Father. And still, in the midst of this joy lies the entire suffering of the Cross, which is not thereby decreased. "If it is possible, let this cup pass from me." These are words of anxiety, which become

10

121

words of abandonment on the Cross. Nevertheless, all the darkness of suffering is, as it were, blotted out and bracketed in the encompassing joy, even when this is the greatest suffering that has ever existed: dying far away from God, carrying all the sins of the world, until the Suffering One, completely crushed by sin, sees neither the end nor the meaning of the agony. There is no answer to the question of the Dying One. The Father cannot allow himself to be heard because he wants to give the Son a perfect joy: the joy of dying in loneliness for him after carrying moment to moment the entire excessive demand of the Passion.

But because we are only human, and sinners as well, we do not experience the separation between joy and suffering in the same way as the Son. We always know, after all, that joy is greater, even when our life is difficult and we are suffering or experiencing sadness. We know that God is absolute joy and that there always remains a place for us right by his side. The brackets that enclose us in suffering are never completely indissoluble. And when we ourselves no longer remember what joy is, we always have the word of Holy Scripture. We can take it and allow it to tell us what joy is. We are never without hope. God can encounter us in his whole light, so that we, out of pure joy, no longer know who we are and what we should do. We look into his perfect joy and are invited to the banquet of this joy. Everything is then carried away by joy, even our worries and hesitations, and even that which is questionable appears to be meaningful. We receive an answer to our Why? and the moment that brings us into the joy of God casts its light over all the days of our life. Heaven and earth have met; the light has shone in our darkness. God did not keep his joy for himself. The Father gives it to the Son and the Spirit, and they return it to him as a gift. In joy the Father also created the world, so that it can participate in his joy. Every man, from first to last, is chosen for and invited into eternity and into its ever-greater joy. He is God's guest with an eternal right of abode in a place where he might think himself to be a stranger.

Sometimes man covers his head and refuses to look and encounter God. God can, however, remove his veil so that it suddenly falls away and we have to look and see what he wants to give us, whether we like it or not. From this moment on, all of our movements are influenced by his light and have their being inside it. We truly begin to see, and the new vision surpasses everything that has been familiar to us until now. All things receive their place and their meaning, and they respond to a hitherto unimagined providence of joy. This includes the task God assigns to us: our mission, our everyday life, and everything else we do and think are now determined by the joy of the triune God. Therefore the believer has to radiate a joyful strength that should not be mistaken for the high spirits of a man who has never encountered God. For the uniqueness of the encounter with God cannot be confused with any other experience. If we really encounter God, this experience continues to live within us.

The Son, who exists on earth in service to the Father, lives with a view to the Father. He lives in a unity with the Father that is also revealed in his unified disposition. He cannot be anything else but what his mission demands from him. But he does not want to be anything else. A Christian who follows the Lord should also be so unified. He cannot afford to live the double life of a man who lives at the same time in joy and reluctance. No one can serve two masters: God and mammon. This sentence shows that a Christian must live in unity, which is a unity of joy. It is that joy which leads us to live on a path of fidelity, trust, and belief, and to remain there. And this is precisely what joy is. For this path leads through the Son to the Father as a way of loving obedience and the fulfillment of eternity in time. It leads through the Son to the Father as a way that the Son has prepared for us so that we can follow it in the joy of grace.

b. *The Objectivity of Joy*

We are accustomed to divide our life into spheres, and we are willing to respect people who belong to these spheres—family, friends, work, and so on— and to arrange a place for them in our life. Those who stand outside remain strangers to us, as if we were able to exercise the commandment of loving our neighbor only in small installments and, moreover, needed to have a certain oversight, as though anything beyond our grasp would be asking too much of us.

If someone personally encounters God, it seems as if he is taken out of his spheres for a moment; their importance recedes strongly into the background. When he returns to them, he has to arrange his relationships in a new way. From now on, he has to share the joy of the encounter, the joy that has become alive within him. This joy comes from a sphere above all other spheres, for God's spheres do not have boundaries. Thus, he will not think even for a moment that he is the only one who has ever encountered God and that he represents a unique point of reference. He knows that God's word transcends time and that many have heard this word before him. He must know as well many who have met God also in his own time. He can visualize that which is personal in his encounter (which is the source of his joy) by looking back at Adam, whom God addressed in paradise. However, he should not tarry with Adam for too long, because the second Adam has come. And he has come certainly not only for him but for all. "For me" is something obligatory, but "for all" is no less so. Already in the Old Testament, God met with many people: with priests, prophets, kings, and with others who were approached by him and received a task. He has to contemplate their obedience and also their disobedience. Finally, he sees the Son and his supreme obedience. He hears what the Son allowed to be laid down in the Scriptures. He contemplates the blowing of the Spirit in the worldwide Church. So he must be satisfied with being one among the many who stand before God. But this modesty is immediately surpassed and turns into the greatest joy when he realizes that it is really he who is meant—he in the midst of his hitherto narrow and fixed spheres. From now on, he is to become all things to all people in the joy of the Lord. He can do this subjectively up to a certain point. Yet, this point is found in a place that he cannot determine, although it certainly exists for him. There is a new measure for his tasks and personal relationships, which is much greater than he thought possible. But even in the fruitfulness of his mission, he cannot go beyond this measure. His days, as all other days, have their end; his strength, too. And still, he will have the strange experience that his time and strength can be extended. But in this experience of expansion, he may become even more aware of his limits than ever before because since his encounter with God he has raised his aims higher than they were previously. He has experienced joy. Whoever has to report on an experience of joy he happened to have will quickly find himself at a loss for words, for he has to refer to something that is extremely personal. He has to describe how he felt when something was taking place. If he uses comparisons in order to liven up his description, they will be unsatisfying most of all to himself.

However, if he prays before God full of joy and thanks him for the gift, then he knows that God fills out every word he says. Indeed, only then does God grant him the understanding of what his word means. Conversation with God is shaped by God himself in such a living way that the one who prays need not worry whether his contribution is worthy of God. God himself will give the fullness. And in this conversation lies a new joy that is a promise of the time to come. The one who prays draws strength from God's inexhaustible source of joy. In their encounter this joy immediately streams forth: the one who prays simply says to God: You see! For God can see and know everything. To say "you see" to those who live around us and to whom we are to communicate our joy is more difficult. And yet, if a Christian truly lives in the joy of his encounter with God, he radiates this joy to those who do not yet believe—who do not yet find strength to throw themselves into the joy of God. And God helps him with this task.

During her feasts and celebrations, the Church proclaims a joyful alleluia. Those who are lukewarm, weak, and unbelieving, who are present only with half their hearts and find themselves in the wrong place, can be seized suddenly by this proclamation and experience more than they want at first to admit.

They were present when Christ's Church rejoiced. And because this Church is the Bride of Christ, her jubilation belongs to the Bridegroom. She rejoices in the joy of the love that is in him and that is allotted to her. This jubilation fills the world to such an extent that it becomes essential and binding for everyone who encounters God. He can see that his own experience corresponds to the experience of the Church. And where his experience threatens to fade and he can hardly recall what jubilation he felt in the moment when he stood before God, there remains next to him the objective jubilation of the Church. As with all other things that come from God, the strength of this joy cannot be measured by man. Once it seemed greater to him than everything else, and that remains the case. The more certain it is, the more genuine it is, and therefore it no longer needs to be felt and experienced to exist as joy. When someone loses the experience of joy, he does not have to invoke it artificially. He remains raised up, together with his joy, toward God. Joy, whether or not it is felt, is finally the same as a contemplative letting be, which has priority over doing. The objective joy of the Church, in which all Christians participate, must be sufficient for them, precisely because in its objectivity it is also *her* joy.

c. The Joy of the Resurrection

The Christian also feels constricted by his earthly life. He sees the limits of his ability, and he reckons with them. And this calculation narrows the whole once again, or it allows him to separate cleanly two aspects of his life: here, everyday existence; there, God and the Church. The two parts do not come together, perhaps because he is afraid of unforeseen consequences. However, if he considers and sees how alive the joy in the Church can be, and if he understands that it is made for him, he can be seized by the grace of joy. His life can be formed in accord with God's will by the Church and by the conclusions of the Christian faith that was given to him. He only has to let everything calculated in advance fall away. If he dares to do this, he discovers something unusual: the Easter joy, which for him is embodied best in sacramental absolution and in the reception of the Lord in the Eucharist, now means something infinitely more to him than in previous years. It is as if he understood for the first time what it means to say: Christ is risen from the dead! What the Lord experienced in those days—the most extreme suffering, the descent into hell, and the Resurrection from the dead—happened just as clearly for him as for the whole Church. There is not one joy for him and a different joy for the Church. *One and the same joy* is given to both: to the Church and to the individual Christian. Without regard for what the individual experiences and endures in the limits of his earthly life and without regard for the self-limitations that he thought necessary, it is given with such a fullness of power that one can sense the divine power in it. At the same time, it is given with such gentleness that no one feels discouraged when he attempts to turn toward this joy personally and to entrust himself to it.

The birth of a new man is a deep mystery, a mystery no less profound than creation itself. Adam and Christ encounter one another, and a Christian stands suddenly at the very place of this encounter, where the second Adam steps into the place of the first Adam and thus redeems him. And a Christian must say Yes to being in this place. In the joy of his own being he must stand before God in such a way that God can bring a new man out of him. Like Adam and Christ, he, too, must be present to the joy of the Father and to make this fatherly joy his own. He must reenact in faith what can only be compared to the Resurrection. As Christ suffered and died for him in order to rise from the dead, so he must experience in himself death and resurrection. A personal death where his sin is, which he considers to be most his own and which he constantly tries to hide from God. He must allow his sin to die, and he has to die to it, so that precisely there God can place the seed of resurrection. He must let himself be purified without shouting: "Stop", even when it is painful at times and goes against all natural inclinations. The purification, however, does not hollow everything out so that nothing remains. It is a preparation for the arrival of the living Lord. The act of belonging to the Lord in communion and the Resurrection of the Lord himself encounter one another exactly at this point where everything was uprooted and sifted. This is the place of fruitfulness.

This new fruitfulness, which leads to the resurrection, does not need any fertilizer or compost; it needs only purity. Such a purity consists of faith, love, and hope, and it is a joyful exchange of giving and receiving. For a loving and a hoping believer, God's word means joy, precisely because it took everything in order now to be able to give everything; and because, from now on, the believer can give something together with the word: joy.

The joy of Christian feasts is always a joy directed toward all; it is a joy that comes from God and goes into the whole world. It is not a joy that can be divided into portions. The parts of joy flow into one another and show their genuineness in the fact that all who approach it recognize each other as individuals who are meant, touched, redeemed, and resurrected. It can happen that someone sees the joy of another and does not understand it. He can, however, receive the other's explanation in such a way that his word becomes alive within him, and he recognizes in himself the other's joy even before he fully understands it. Indeed, he also believes before he has understood everything. Saying Yes before one fully understands can be learned from Mary's Yes, which is a word of joy, a word leading to all the sacraments, and a word to the triune God. It is indeed so much a Yes of joy that the Church is not merely nourished by a vague realization of what has occurred; rather, she takes it in, possesses it, and considers it to be her own because Mary bequeathed it to her and because it has been believed and carried out by the Church without interruption from that moment on. In this Yes we find something of God, who calls for it; and something of man, who achieves it.

11

Truth

a. Conversion and Truth

For a Christian, it goes without saying that God lives within his Church. But this thought can put him to sleep: God is here for the whole; he provides an order for all; he enacts laws through the Church, behind which he, as it were, disappears. One can hold onto letters and thus forget the spirit a little. One does more or less what is required, without committing oneself too much. It is as though the commandment of love of God and neighbor were a natural convention out of which certain rules of conduct arise for times and situations that are sufficient to live by.

However, a Christian can also encounter God suddenly in prayer, in an inspiration, during liturgy, or in some human situation, and now he is addressed personally. He, and no other, is meant. This encounter does not concern formulated laws that can be kept easily; it concerns love, genuineness, and this Christ who says about himself that he is the truth. And the truth is also the way and the life.

If God becomes true in this way, then the Christian also becomes true in a new sense. He can no longer separate his own truth from his way and his life; rather, he has to adapt his truth on his life's path to God's truth. God took hold of him during this encounter—by which end is irrelevant, because God will not let him go until the whole person follows after and subordinates his truth and his way of life to God's.

He must reckon with God's truth as the first factor. He has to make it present to himself in prayer. He knows that he cannot handle it, but it will handle him. So he has to examine everything that he has done and thought until now in light of this truth. Will it pass the test? Will it prove to be true? The expression "true" is given an incredible intensity, for God himself is the Truth. In this test a Christian will become meek, for it seems that most of what he has done will not pass. There is hardly anything that he could declare valid. He understands that he is a sinner. Until now he has forgotten God; he did not love his neighbors in a Christian way. In these or similar succinct statements he exhausts what he is able to say about himself. And yet, God in his truth has reached him; he has found something in him that makes him endearing to God, but hardly endearing in the state in which God found him—at best in the state of truth for which he strives. God has to continue giving his own truth until the recipient becomes a servant of this truth. He lives off a foreign good, the divine good, in order to become a partner

for God. He should find himself at home in this good
that is not his and so recognize in it the gift meant
to be his own.

When he prays, he feels overwhelmed by the newness of divine truth. When he works, he understands
that, here too, this truth forces itself on him time and
time again. Repeatedly, something new arrives that
can be expressed in a simple formula: God's truth!
It has no criterion other than the one given by God
himself, insofar as he is. There are many paths upon
which a believer can walk in order to grasp something, not as his own, but as divine truth and to find
therein life for himself. God is so much the truth
that he has the power to fill to the brim the most
varied lives, to bring the right content out of every
form, and to transform all appearance into reality. If
the one who prays takes Scripture in his hands in order to meditate upon Jesus' life, verse after verse, he
will be constantly amazed at God's truth, its true demands, and true realization. He will be amazed even
more at the fact that the stories and parables address,
no longer just anyone, but me myself. God speaks
to me out of the absolute. I cannot, while listening,
relativize what he says; rather I must acknowledge
the absolute as valid for me. This means that I must
allow it to become true for me. It is not the opinions
of a faraway time, opinions tailored to our age, that
are being expressed; nor is a foreign language being
spoken that would require translation. And further:

God is not divisible. When he describes himself as truth and he gives himself to us as truth, then it is not in drops, but wholly. The light of his truth does not allow itself to be dimmed for the weak-sighted.

But since the divine truth is at the same time absolute love, this truth never has the character of something impossible or unreasonable, even where it seems merciless in its exigency. Love is always possible, and it always finds its way through. When Christ says about himself that he is the truth, he does so as God who became man, who is now Son of Man in order precisely as such to confirm the truth of this statement. For God's truth is his faithful love in his covenant with man, and he proclaims this truth insofar as he accomplishes the act of salvation. Who could fail to see the truth of this love on the Cross?

In the same way, each sacrament instituted by the Lord also contains truth as its primordial characteristic—a truth that is new at each reception and yet rests in the ancient truth of the Word. The miracle of the bread becoming the Body and of the wine becoming the Blood is a miracle of truth; it is the presence of the incarnate God. Perhaps a sinner who encounters the miracle of the Eucharist is so overwhelmed by it that he, as it were, helplessly believes it, without finding any access for himself. The sacrament of confession can help him. Here he has a measure: he knows the genuineness of his confession, the truth of his sin, and the weight of his past life. If he receives

absolution, this past truth dies out. The truth is now
what is to come, that he can begin a new life. This
arrival testifies to the strength of his truth precisely
in that it was able to wipe away his past. A strength
has manifested itself in the one confessing that he
scarcely would have believed just moments before.
He confessed out of a need to receive forgiveness;
but only in the event of this forgiveness does he realize how enormous the truth of absolution is, how
it liberates him, and how widely it opens for him a
path to a new life of truth.

b. *Living from the Truth*

We judge our neighbors in everyday life. If, however,
we meet one of them in Church during Holy Mass,
in front of the confessional, or at the Communion
rail, then our critique must be silenced. This man is
doing something that corresponds to the acknowledg-
ment of truth. He is here in order to encounter God,
in order to do faithfully in the Church what countless generations of believers have done before him: to
worship the true God. He is kneeling with his hands
folded, in the posture of humility. He expresses the
truth, which he perhaps forgets occasionally in his
everyday life or to which he does not fully correspond. But he will not be able to forget this attitude
completely. It endures not only because the Church

as such remains living, but also because man, in spite
of all his faults, does not want to deny his faith in
his everyday life. He wants to carry something inside
himself that can somehow be shared, perhaps without his being aware of it. God's truth does not allow
itself to be diluted. It is strong enough to remain itself even when individuals testify to this truth in a
weak and a lukewarm way.

If a man encounters God, for example, in the sense
of a conversion from non-belief to belief or a "rever-
sion" from a purely formal faith to a real faith, he is
penetrated by a truth that liberates him and shows him
a path. It frees him up to follow the path. The truth is
Christ, and the path toward him is now open. Until
now, man was like someone who knew by hearsay
that something existed behind a door that was locked.
Now the door is opened: nothing impedes his view
of the truth. To be sure, this truth is infinite, which
means it cannot be immediately grasped. It remains
a kingdom that will be inexhaustible for the whole
of eternity, eternally opening up in new ways. It will
open not only in incidental aspects, but out of the
heart of truth, for the infinite God is able to shine
forth even in infinity. When a convert looks into
this truth, it is difficult for him to see that others do
not believe because they do not find courage or because the testimony of truth seems to them to en-
tail too many difficulties. He will also have to admit,
however, that the truth, which is one with love, is

so strong that it can take responsibility for leaving men in the difficulties of faith. These difficulties can never be as essential as the character of divine truth itself. The fruit of God's truth and love will constantly accompany even the imperfect believer or the believer who believes for impure reasons. Although often veiled, misused, and betrayed, it will still lead men untiringly toward the right, and it will correct his straying. Divine truth gives to men not only the sense for what is right, but also the fruit of and the path to what is right.

John of the Cross, who can no longer see any trace of God in the dark night, who carries within himself a burning faith whose fruitfulness he does not see and who would like to throw himself to the ground because of love and is restrained by his desolation, is, with regard to truth, just like a child who says his simple prayer from his heart. Similarly, the truth of God is indivisible, and God always offers truth to man as a viable path. With regard to his behavior toward God, no one can say that he could just as well have done something completely different and contrary. If once he set out upon a path for his life that God showed him, then later there is no longer any chance to go "either this way or that", not even in smaller decisions. The path of truth is clear and transparent, perhaps not at the moment when we follow it, but later. It is as transparent as God's will, which at times may not be completely clear for the individual. Nevertheless, this will is made clear to him through the official instruction of the Church. This instruction is a guiding principle for the individual, who is himself searching for the way of truth. He will discover in prayer which path is his, even when he is unable to check its correctness at every step. In rare cases, his path can be made immediately clear. In most cases, however, he has to entrust himself to God through the Church in such a way that, with the gift of his person, he surrenders everything that could count as reassurance along the way of truth.

In truth there is from time to time a battle between the individual and the Church: a tugging back and forth that appears to have no center. The center is never, of course, a place of lukewarmness; it is the narrow path. The center is the Yes that has just been pronounced. If we try to see this center together with Mary, then it is clear that her Yes was pronounced in the narrow place of her meeting with the angel, in love and the fullness of obedience. The moment it is pronounced, however, it expands so much that no center or narrow path is visible anymore, but only the overflowing fullness of the whole divine truth. And this is the widest path, upon which walk the Mother of the Lord, all the angels and saints, all the faithful of the Old and New Covenants, and all who somehow fulfill God's will. Only when she entered was the path narrow: it was the I-thou relationship between

Mary and the angel, who brought her God's Word. This narrow place reveals the inevitability of the I-thou relation between God and man. Here all truth comes together in order to expand from here through the Church into the fullness of all redeemed creation, indeed, into the fullness of eternal life, which once stood on the narrowest path, on the point of the moment and of the Yes.

c. Sacramental Truth

When a man wants to make a statement about truth, he can take into his hands the first object he sees and say: "As truly as this exists . . ." and then continue with a comparison. This statement has, however, a limited duration. The object can be moved, changed, or destroyed. Its truth is bound up with time. If it concerns more distant things, the statement can become more difficult; it needs more words; it would have to link together concepts, ideas, and memories. Though I have an overview of the connections and can count on them with confidence, I can make them intelligible to others only with effort. I soon encounter objections regarding my one-sided and subjective point of view or my way of linking things together. They will relativize my truth.

When, however, Jesus Christ says: I am the truth, then the word "truth" receives a greatness far beyond all of this. He, the Son of God, and the absolute truth coincide. A fanatic is someone who has discovered a small truth and reduces everything else to this truth. He knows this one truth; what does not match, what does not fit in, does not exist. He can be ready to lay down his life for this truth of his, to separate himself from his best friends, to do things that he finds completely repugnant. In relation to his truth, he has become a *thing*. When, however, Christ says: I am the truth, when he comes to redeem the world as the truth, then no fanaticism in relation to him is possible. Man, who is redeemed through him, does not become a thing in relation to him. He receives, in truth, space: a way and a life, freedom to walk in Christ's truth to the truth of the Father.

But Christ returns to heaven after death and the Resurrection. He has to leave traces on earth that are truthful in the same way that he is, so that those who follow him will not get lost and so that his truth will remain living within them. Thus the future saints and the faithful members of his Church do not find less support than what the apostles had in him. This support, this extension of the truth that he himself is, can be found in the first place in the sacraments of the Church, which are all truthful expressions of God's truth. God consecrates and blesses as he did on earth. He baptizes and hears confessions; he gives his Body and Blood; he bestows his Holy Spirit; and he does all this as an expression of his being true. Each sacramental act is an extension of God's truth, which does not, however, lose anything of its power. As true as this sacrament is, so true is God! The forms of expression can be ordinary human forms. Now, however, man does not grasp just any object in order to compare truth with it. He takes hold of truth itself in the Spirit of truth—who comes from God, and when God gives the Spirit, he gives himself. Earthly truthfulness has a perpetual correspondence, a point of reference in God. As an earthly act, Communion consists in eating and drinking, but this act corresponds to a participation in the divine truth: not only in the act of faith, but also in the act of receiving into the mouth and swallowing, the complete reception into oneself. This is an act, not only of love, but first of all of a sober, dry obedience in relation to truth, an act of submitting to it. Whoever does this acknowledges God's truth as his greatest teacher. Since God is the truth, everything he establishes and orders is true. And the Church is here to bear witness to this truth. She preserves the truth; she receives it in order to give it away. She administers it in accord with God. As a sprinter carries a torch from one place to another so that a new torch can be ignited there, so the sacraments receive the substance of the true God —his Body and his Spirit and also his Word—in order to ignite by it new faith and new love, which keep God's truth alive on earth. It is certainly also alive in Scripture, alive in heaven, where God's will alone reigns, and also alive in the Church and within each Christian, despite his faults and shortcomings. And it is so because the sacramental reality constantly lifts man up above his own level onto the level of the divine truth.

Because the mystery of the sacraments is one with the mystery of God's truth, and because the inviolability of the sacraments comes from the divine truth, they cannot be damaged, weakened, or falsified by our lukewarmness, lack of understanding, and sin. The power of the ever-constant newness of the Eucharist, the power of each absolution (which comes undiminished from the Cross), the power of each baptism as a beginning of the eternal life in time, the power of each confirmation (which transforms an immature person into a mature one), this power is one with God himself. There are many different sacraments, but their origin is one and the same. They are like different life preservers that are being thrown to a drowning man from the same shore.

One who feels touched by God and is uncertain about what he should believe could find the teaching of our Lord, on the one hand, too easy: indeed, every child can grasp it; it does not look like a divine mystery. On the other hand, he could complain that the teaching is too hard, for each simple word constantly opens up new and mysterious horizons; each step of discipleship brings with it other countless steps, and there is no end in sight to being a Christian. For the life of faith consists of so many things that we do not like to do, things we would scarcely choose if we foresaw them already in the beginning. Too easy and too hard: but both balance each other in the sacramental life and in the objective life of the Church. Both are aspects of God's truth from which nothing can be taken away and to which nothing can be added. God gives us this truth as a whole, and we can always see only certain facets. These, however, come together to form a whole, and we cannot separate them out from the whole. The diamond sparkles only when all its edges remain as they are. Certainly, we can look at only one single surface by itself, but we have to realize that it is an aspect of the whole and that it reveals itself for the sake of the whole. All the aspects together, however, reveal a single thing: that the eternal God communicates himself to us in his truth as a whole, so that also we can give ourselves to him as a whole.

d. Opening to God

God allows man to encounter him so that man can find joy and truth in God. And if man is often convinced of his own nothingness during the very first encounter he has with God, then this first insight only prepares the ground for what is to come. Man renounces the idea of debating with God, of forcing him into a partnership in which he could continually place his word on the scale against God's word. He has recognized once and for all that God is superior to him. But he has also realized how close God drew to him through the Incarnation of his Son in order to open for him a way toward God. And each new encounter will have the sense of an urgent invitation. If he, however, has said his "Lord, I am not worthy", he will no longer waste any time thinking about his own unworthiness and becoming obsessed with it. On the contrary, he will open himself in order to allow God, who is the only one who is worthy, to enter. From now on, he will fix his gaze on God's truth, and he will let himself be led by it. It is a guidance of the child by the father. It will be, in most cases, something absolutely simple and direct —an examination of man by God, a demand that he separate himself ever more decisively from his sin —but always a guidance into the truth, which is so great that it leaves space for every joy. The one who encounters God cannot say that he was looking for his happiness. At most he can claim that he desired truth and received it in abundance. And everything that belongs to it, also the happiness of being a child of God, everything will be given to him, not *next to* the truth, but *in* the truth. For all of God's gifts belong to the grace of his self-revelation, and all of them want to transform man to a true image of the true God, to an appropriate response to the call of God that has reached him.

Man's response to God's truth cannot be an always new questioning and examining of this truth. The truth is here; the Church has tested it. God has made himself sufficiently known; the response must be a leap into the ever-greater truth. And the one who is making the leap experiences that there is always much more at stake here than he expected. God, who once revealed himself to man, never draws back into the inaccessible and the abstract. He gives himself to man ever more concretely in the Eucharist, in all the sacraments of the Church, and in all the words of the Scriptures. And a Christian can meet God again in an ever more living way in his neighbors as well. On all the paths of his life, eternal love comes to meet him in a very real way so that he can no longer cease to worship.